Rock Climbing For the Absolute Beginners

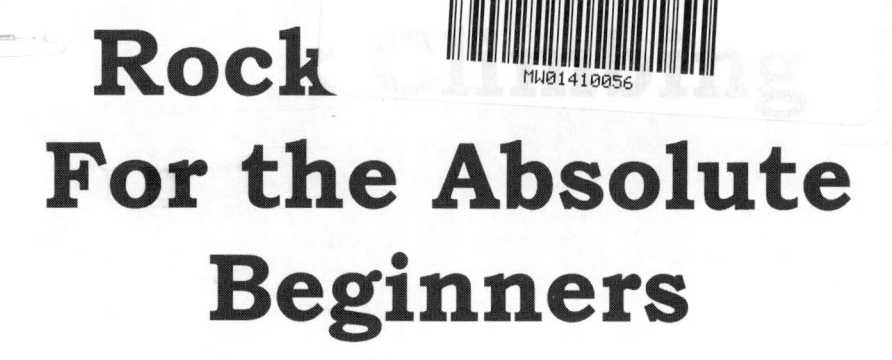

A Complete Guide to Bouldering, Mountaineering, Top-Rope & Trad Climbing- Includes Knot Tying Tutorials

By

K.J. Moore

Copyrighted Material

Copyright © Autumn Leaf Publishing Press, 2019

Email: Publisher@AutumnLeafPub@gmail.com

All Rights Reserved.

Without limiting the rights under the copyright laws, no part of this publication may be reproduced, stored in or introduced into a retrieval system, or transmitted, in any form or by any means (electronic, mechanical, photocopying, recording or otherwise), without the prior written consent of the publisher of this book.

Autumn Leaf Publishing Press publishes its books and guides in a variety of electronic and print formats, Some content that appears in print may not be available in electronic format, and vice versa.

AUTUMN LEAF
PUBLISHING PRESS

Design & Illustration by Rebecca Johnson

First Edition

Contents

The Climb 9

Starting Out 16

    What to Expect 20

    Types of Climbing 22

        Bouldering 23

        Top-Rope Climbing 24

        Sport Climbing 26

        Traditional Climbing 28

Learn the Lingo 31

    Climbing Terminology 31

    Understanding Climbing Communication 41

        Belay Commands 41

        Climbing Commands 43

        Descent Commands 44

        Using the Terms 45

Understanding Climbing Grades 47

    Grading a Climb 47

    Grading Systems for Bouldering 48

Climbing Etiquette...51
Gear Up..53
  Shoes...54
    Selecting Shoes 55
    Proper Use of Shoes 56
    Caring for Your Shoes 57
    Safety Inspection 58
  Harness 59
    Selecting a Harness 60
    Proper Use of a Harness..............................63
    Caring for a Harness....................................65
    Safety Inspection 66
  Chalk and Chalk Bag 67
    Selecting Chalk 68
    Selecting a Chalk Bag 70
    Proper Use of Chalk and Bag......................71
    Hand Care 73
  Belay Device 74
    Selecting a Belay Device 75
    Proper Use of a Belay Device 77

Caring for a Belay Device..................................79

  Safety Inspection..79

Carabiners..80

  Selecting Carabiners 81

  Proper Use of Carabiners 84

  Caring for Carabiners 84

  Safety Inspection..85

Helmet...86

  Selecting a Helmet..87

  Proper Use of Helmets....................................88

  Caring for Helmets..88

  Safety Inspection..89

Climbing Rope..89

  Selecting Rope 90

  Proper Use of Rope 94

  Caring for Rope 95

  Safety Inspection..96

Crash Pads 97

  Selecting Crash Pads.......................................97

  Proper Use of Crash Pads........................... 100

- Caring for Crash Pads 100
- Safety Inspection 101
- Climbing Clothing 101
- Concluding Advice about Equipment 102
- Knots & Anchors 103
  - Climbing Knots 103
    - Figure-Eight Follow-Through 105
    - Figure-Eight on a Bight 112
    - Stopper Knot 114
    - Clove Hitch 118
    - Climbing Knot Safety 121
  - Climbing Anchors 122
    - Natural Anchors 123
    - Fixed Anchors 124
    - Removable Anchors 125
- Climbing Technique 128
  - Handholds 129
  - Footholds 134
  - Movements 135
  - Last Words about Technique 139

Training to Climb 141

    Warming Up 142

    Upper Body Training 143

    Hand Strengthening 145

    Lower Body Training 147

    Endurance 148

    Balance 149

    Getting Your Mind Right 150

    Fear of Falling 151

    A Note on Training 152

Climbing Safety 154

    Rope Check 155

    Harness Check 156

    Knot Check 157

    Helmet Check 158

    Device Check 159

    Climbing Communication 160

    Safely Falling 161

Transitioning to Outdoor Climbs 164

    Environment 165

Fear Factor 166

Gear 168

Grades 169

Helmet 170

Holds 171

Respect Nature (and Each Other) 171

Last Word about Outdoor Climbing 172

Advancing Your Climbing Skills 173

Going to the Next Level 174

Climb 174

Yearn to Learn 175

Push Yourself 176

Try Different Styles 176

Continuing Education 177

Conclusion 179

The Climb

Heart racing, legs trembling, palms damp with sweat, you cling to the side of the wall in search of the next hold, the next foot placement that will advance you higher.

You catch a glimpse of the distance below as your brain confronts you with all of the things that could go wrong.

"What if I fall?"

With every move you fight against your mind, every cell in your body screaming. This fierce passion and thrill of a rush, expressed through climbing, is what draws many to the intense sport of rock climbing, yet leaves others scratching their heads.

What could be the benefit of such a dangerous feat? Why climb?

Climbing is considered a movement across vertical terrain using your hands and feet. On a basic level, climbing is a fundamental human need.

Before the modern age, our predecessors spent time scrambling over rough terrain in search of their next meal. They scurried up mountains and trees to survey land.

Evidence of this fundamental need is found on playgrounds where children swing from monkey bars, hang from jungle gyms, climb over rocks, and up trees.

We forgot how to climb.

However, it seems that as we become adults, we unlearn how to climb.

Instead, we have sedentary office jobs or spend the weekends on the couch binge-watching reality television.

While it would be nice to capture a concrete answer to the question "why do we climb," the truth is the reason is as varied as each climber.

Some climb for the benefits of a demanding full-body workout, requiring the use of muscles you may not know you have.

Some climb as a casual hobby, others for the love of the outdoors, the thrill of an excellent adventure, the call of the wild.

It's NEVER too late to learn.

Whether you want to climb for one of these reasons or all of these reasons, it is never too late to learn, but do not be fooled. Rock climbing will not come without its challenges.

Climbing is physically demanding and requires endurance and muscle building. While you may not necessarily need brute strength, it will require lots of desire and enthusiasm.

Climbing requires precise focus and critical thinking, the unity of mind and body, as you determine where to place your foot or which hold to grab. It requires patience and practice, and for many, it requires conquering the biggest challenge of all – a fear of heights.

Despite feeling like a withering pile of nerves while ascending the wall, climbing has numerous benefits. As previously mentioned, rock climbing is a killer workout. Some studies show that you can burn roughly 800 calories for every hour that you climb, a number that only increases as your level of climbing experience increases.

It improves your flexibility through an increased range of motion.

It builds endurance, strengthens, and tones muscles. While not entirely a form of cardio, it is likely to get your heart pumping.

> *For many, climbing is a spiritual exercise, much like yoga or meditation.*

Rock climbing has been shown to boost brain function through the use of problem-solving and body awareness.

It reduces stress by increasing levels of the hormone norepinephrine, which helps the brain respond to stress.

It is entirely reasonable to feel nervous or anxious about learning to climb, especially given there are many disciplines of climbing that include:

- Mountaineering
- Ice climbing
- Free-solo
- Crack climbing
- Sport
- Traditional
- Top-rope climbing
- Bouldering

For this guide, we will focus on top-rope climbing and bouldering. While some will be more anxious and nervous than others, it is essential and imperative for safety for you to be patient with yourself.

Climbing is a process; you will find new confidence as you gain experience and progress. Climbing is experiencing new places, allowing you to behold breathtaking views from places mostly inaccessible.

It will enable you to walk the edge of comfort zones and conquer fears. It quite literally gives meaning to the phrase "reaching new heights."

Beginner climbers must always use sound judgment, as they are the most at risk for accidents. Redundancy is a must to prevent accidents.

Always check and then double-check all climbing systems. Always use gear properly as it is intended. Use equipment rated for climbing.

Be proactive and avoid injury by removing any jewelry or accessories that could catch on the rock. Never attempt to climb beyond your ability and skill level and never rely solely on books and tutorials to learn.

For your safety, and the security of your

climbing partner, always seek help from a qualified climbing expert.

* * * * * *

Heart racing, legs trembling, palms damp with sweat, you cling to the side of the wall in search of the next hold, the next foot placement that will advance you higher. You catch a glimpse of the distance below as your brain confronts you with all the things that could go wrong.

"What if I fall?"

With every move you fight against your mind, every cell in your body screaming. You reach the top; your tiny size put into context against the giant walls.

You feel powerful, humbled, free. In this inspired instant, you realize that it is not always about the climb itself, but what you learned about yourself on the way up.

Starting Out

Climbing is considered to be a dangerous and intensely technical sport, therefore mastering the basics is a crucial first step. Fortunately, there are many options for learning and familiarizing yourself with the sport of rock climbing.

If you do not know an experienced climber, an indoor climbing gym or health club facility is an ideal place to learn. Many local indoor gyms offer beginner classes in which they give an introduction and fundamental lessons for a small fee.

Depending on where you live, another option might be sports and outdoor recreation stores like REI (https://www.rei.com).

These stores offer classes and clinics for new climbers as well as courses for more advanced climbers.

Depending on the class options available, climbing classes taken through sports and recreation stores may teach climbing either indoors or outdoors.

Speaking from experience, I find it highly beneficial to learn from a local indoor rock climbing gym. Climbing gyms are becoming more popular in several cities.

They offer a safe, controlled environment in which to learn the basics under the supervision of experienced staff members.

Basic classes commonly include how to choose shoes, using and adjusting a harness for proper fit, tying-in, and how to belay.

Essentially, "belaying" is learning to use rope and climbing devices to help others climb safely.

Additionally, you will discover various terminology to help you understand climbing jargon.

While not preferred by everyone, learning indoors can be advantageous for the new climber, as well as being less intimidating.

Climbing indoors makes you stronger for when you are ready to transition to climbing outdoors.

Indoor gyms are easily accessible, and they provide the comfort of spongy-soft floors and prefabricated walls.

Handholds and footholds are bolted onto the wall, forming routes up the walls which are periodically reset to avoid climbing the same path over and over.

Indoor walls can range from 20 to 50 feet in height with smooth slabs or overhanging arches.

Depending on the types of climbing available, you will likely find top-rope climbing, sport climbing, and small walls for bouldering.

Some gyms offer walls with an auto-belay device, allowing the climber to ascend the wall without needing a partner to belay.

Except for bouldering, which does not require the use of ropes, all of these forms of climbing utilize rope and harness for maximum safety.

Climbing gyms offer a social environment, a chance to meet and observe others within the climbing community, or find a climbing partner. It allows you to not only learn the basics but the ability to practice specialized moves and techniques in a structured environment.

Indoor climbing comes with the added benefit of not requiring you to own gear.

A gym usually provides the equipment necessary for climbing.

This essential equipment will include climbing shoes, a harness, chalk/chalk bag, and in some cases, carabiners and belay devices.

What to Expect

When looking for classes to get you started, courses like "rope 101," "up-rope," or "belay 101" will be catered to the beginner.

Sessions can range from $40 and upwards of $140 depending on how involved the course is.

These classes commonly provide you with gear for the duration of the lesson. Once you have signed up, you will be required to sign a waiver. Although climbing gyms are generally safe, accidents can still sometimes happen if you are careless.

You can expect, at a minimum, a two-hour introductory class. The first portion of the course generally takes place in a classroom setting. The second half of the course allows hands-on experience as you prepare yourself to climb and then actually climb.

As the climber, you will learn how to properly adjust your harness and tie-in so that you can climb safely. You will also learn how to belay and use belay devices, that is, holding and securing the other end of the line for the climber so that they will not fall.

> **Courses also include learning the proper terminology so that you and your climbing partner can effectively communicate.**

Although not entirely necessary, you may find it easier to bring along a friend with interest in climbing. Climbing is a social sport and generally requires two people - the climber and the person on belay.

If all your friends are scared of heights, auto-belay devices will allow you to climb alone. However, only climbing with an auto-belay will not allow for the practice often needed with tying-in and belaying.

> **Do not be afraid to introduce yourself; climbing gyms and communities are mostly friendly places.**

Although fellow climbers may seem intimidating, they are likely just focused, but more than happy to answer your questions and provide tips.

Whether you would like to occasionally climb as a hobby or advance your skills to learn lead climbing, indoor climbing is sure to get your climbing career off the ground.

Next, we will take a look at the different types of climbing to help you get an idea of where to start and where you might like to go.

Types of Climbing

Many forms of climbing exist, and this can result in a novice climber feeling overwhelmed.

Let us take a look at some different types of climbing to help get an idea of where to start.

Bouldering

Bouldering is a term used to describe climbing short, challenging routes on small rock faces or blocks of rock. These routes are usually no higher than 20 feet. These routes are called "problems."

Bouldering offers a simple climbing experience in terms of gear, as it does not require a harness or ropes. Shoes, chalk/chalk bag, and one or more crash pads are all that is needed to get you started.

Bouldering makes you stronger and allows you to practice climbing moves while being safely just above the ground.

If you plan to boulder outdoors, make sure to borrow, rent, or buy a crash pad or two for safety. Crash pads are made from thick foam and help cushion a rough landing.

Top-Rope Climbing

Top-rope climbing is considered the safest way for beginners to learn. Top-roping means ascending walls with a rope fixed to an anchor above the climber. The line runs from the belay person on the ground through the top anchor and back down to the climber. This method is similar to a pulley system.

Should the climber take a fall, utilizing a top anchor allows the person on belay to arrest and hold the climber by locking off the rope.

This technique creates a safe climbing environment by protecting the climber in the event of a fall.

Top-rope climbing requires the necessary equipment as mentioned earlier - shoes, a harness, chalk/chalk bag, a carabiner, a belay device, and rope. When climbing indoors, anchors are fixed and ready for the climber to tie-in and the belay person to setup.

Most large climbing gyms offer auto-belay devices.

Auto-belay devices do not require a belay

person. Instead, you can climb alone.

To use an auto-belay method, you merely clip-in and climb.

When you are ready to come down, sit back into your harness and walk your legs down the wall as the auto-belay device lowers you safely to the ground.

If you are learning to climb outdoors, top anchors may not be fixed in place, requiring you to learn how to set anchors.

Sport Climbing

Sport climbing is a type of lead climbing that uses pre-bolted anchors that are placed into the rock by trained professionals.

The bolts are drilled into the rock so that they become permanent metal fixtures.

This climbing style emphasizes athletic movement and pushing one's limits by trying more challenging routes, all while maintaining a relatively safe climbing environment.

Sport climbing requires, at minimum, the essential equipment as well as carabiners and quickdraws, a belay device, and rope.

A quickdraw, which is a vital tool for sport climbing, allows the climber the ability to clip the rope into each bolt as they follow a predetermined route.

This style of climbing enables the climber to concentrate more on movement and figuring out difficult areas.

Many indoor gyms offer sport climbing walls.

Also, it is relatively easy for the urban outdoor climber to locate bolted crags in nearby popular hiking spots.

Traditional Climbing

Traditional climbing, more commonly called "trad" climbing, refers to the climber placing their own removable protection gear as they climb.

Protection gear consists of cams, nuts, and wedges, in addition to the essential equipment like shoes, a harness, chalk/chalk bag, rope, carabiners, and belay devices.

Trad climbers place belay anchors and do not generally use bolts.

To be a trad climber requires more skill than sport climbing since the climber is responsible for determining the route up, creating anchors, and placing protective gear.

Climbers must learn to be skilled in knowing anchor systems and how to evaluate anchor sites.

Trad climbing is also more of an investment in terms of gear, as you will need to invest in equipment referred to as a "rack."

A rack includes a collection of protection anchors, quickdraws, and slings that are carried up the route to build the protection system.

Due to the nature of this style of climbing, trad climbers tend to scale large walls such as the El Capitan in Yosemite Valley.

Other types of climbing include mountaineering or alpine climbing and ice climbing.

In mountaineering or alpine climbing, the climber scales mountain peaks using both rock and ice climbing techniques.

These are the climbers who scale Mount

Everest and similar terrain.

Ice climbing is climbing where very skilled climbers ascend ice walls and gullies and even frozen waterfalls with the help of ice tools.

Learn the Lingo

When you regularly hang around other climbers, you learn they speak a language entirely their own.

You are sure to learn at least ten new climbing vocabulary words with each trip to the gym.

While by no means a comprehensive list, this glossary will help you on your way to using and understanding some of the most common climbing terminology and commands.

Climbing Terminology

Anchor - A safety system at the top of a pitch, or any temporary or permanent attachment to the rock, used to protect the climber against falls. Anchors may come in many forms such as trees, boulders, and chockstones, to name a few.

Backstep – Stepping on the outside edge of the climbing shoe while having the hip against the rock.

Belay – Holding and managing the rope that the climber is tied onto to lower, maintain, and catch a falling climber.

Belayer – The person in charge of the climber's rope. The person on belay takes or feeds the line as the climber ascends the wall. The belayer is also in charge of lowering and catching a falling climber.

Belay anchor – An anchor used to secure a belay station.

Belay station – The location from which the belayer conducts the belaying or uses a belay device. The belayer is commonly anchored to the floor or terrain.

Belay device – One of several devices attached to the harness, used to lower and hold a climber's fall. The rope runs through the device to the climber.

Belay loop – A loop of sewn webbing on the front of a rock climbing harness, used as the attachment point for rappel and belay devices.

Beta – Helpful information about moves or strategies, protection, and the approach to a climb, generally given before or during the climb to help the climber's ascent.

Bight – A bend or loop of rope that does not cross itself, used for creating knots and threading through a belay or rappel device.

Bolt – A permanent metal anchor set into a drilled hole.

Bomber – Refers to a completely reliable and secure anchor or piece of gear so strong it could withstand a bomb blast. Also referred to as "bombproof."

Bouldering – Climbing boulders or short cliffs without a rope, usually close to the ground.

Bounce step – A move initiated by bouncing off your lower foot.

Brake hand – The hand that holds the rope to catch a falling climber. This hand NEVER leaves the rope.

Brake strand – The strand of rope located on the brake hand side of the belay device.

Carabiner – An oval, pear, or D-shaped high-strength aluminum or steel snap-link used to connect parts of the climbing system, as well as connecting climbers to the rope safety system.

Chalk – Powdered gymnastic chalk used by climbers to absorb moisture and sweat to help keep the climber's hands from slipping.

Class – A rating system from one to six describing the terrain a climber might face.

Cleaning – Refers to the act of removing protection anchors from a climb.

Crack climbing – A climbing style that uses cracks in the rock for hand and footholds.

Crag – Slang that refers to a climbing wall.

Cragging – Slang that refers to the act of climbing a wall.

Coil – A bend or loop in rope or webbing that crosses over itself.

Crimp – A small edge hold that is grabbed with fingers bent at the middle joint.

Crimping – The act of grabbing a small edge using a crimp, sometimes only with the pads of the fingers.

Crux – The hardest move or series of moves on a route or pitch.

Dyno – An upward thrust where the climber pushes on the footholds and pulls on the handholds to generate momentum. This momentum allows the climber to "jump" upward to catch a distant hold.

Edging – A foot position that uses the inside or the outside edge of the shoe on footholds.

Fall factor – Measures the severity of a fall by dividing the length of fall by the length of rope in the system. The higher the fall factor, the greater the force on the anchors, the climber, and the belayer.

Figure-eight knot – A knot shaped like a number eight, used for tying the rope into the harness, tying two ropes together, and tying a loop for anchors or haul packs.

Fixed protection – Any permanent anchor point or gear left permanently in the rock.

Footwork – Refers to how to use your feet on different types of footholds.

Grade – A rating system that indicates the difficulty of a climb. Several systems exist and vary depending on the type of climbing. Some systems also suggest how long a climb will take to complete, ranging from hours to several days.

Grigri – A type of auto-locking belay device.

Guide hand – The hand opposite the brake hand that is used to position and manage the rope.

Highball – A tall boulder problem with a potentially dangerous fall.

High-stepping – Reaching the foot to a higher foothold, waist level, or higher.

Horn – A spike projection of rock that can be used for an anchor or a hold.

Jamming – Refers to the act of placing hands or feet in a crack to create a hold.

Jug – A large handhold, similar to a jug handle, that you can wrap your whole hand around.

Leader – The first person to lead a climb. The leader assumes the most risk.

Lead climbing – The first person to climb up a pitch while placing protection along the route.

Lowering – Descending from a climb by hanging on the rope and being lowered by the belayer.

Natural protection – An anchor made from a natural feature such as a tree or boulder.

Overhang – A segment of rock that is steeper than vertical.

Pinch grip – A handhold where the fingers and thumb work opposite of one another to pinch a hold.

Pitch – The section of a climb between belay stations. The length of a pitch is determined by the length of the rope, as well as the location of ledges used for belays.

Pocket – A hole in the rock that forms a hand or foothold. This type of hold allows the climber to fit a finger or two or the tips of the toes into the hole.

Rappel – A method of using the rope to lower yourself from a high point where you cannot otherwise safely descend without the use of protection.

Rope drag – Friction on the rope caused by the cord running over rock and through carabiners and protection pieces. Rope drag increases with each bend in the line.

Slopers – Refers to holds that slope towards you. Slopers can be difficult to grab onto, requiring the climber to palm them.

Side pull – A vertically oriented handhold, usually requiring the climber to lean against the hold to be able to use it.

Scrambling – Refers to the act of climbing without a rope, using the hands and feet. Scrambling is an ambiguous term that can range from meaning trekking up steep terrain to purely hiking.

Smear – A foothold where the entire front of the shoe's sole is pressed against a section of rock where no proper footing exists. The friction of the shoe's rubber and the climber's body weight allows the climber to stand.

Soloing – Climbing a route without a rope. This term may also be called "free soloing" and is often fatal in the event of a fall.

Spotting – Protecting a climber who is bouldering by helping to control a fall. The spotter stands on the ground behind the climber and helps to steer the falling climber to a safe landing zone, like a crash pad.

Standing end – Refers to the opposite end of the rope from the one the climber is tied.

Tail – The section of rope that sticks out after tying a knot.

Toe-in – Stepping straight onto a pocket or tiny edge with the toe of the shoe.

Top-rope anchor – The belay anchor, used for a top-rope.

Topo – A map of a route that provides information by using symbols to show features like cracks, overhangs, ledges, belays, fixed protection, and ratings.

Traverse – Refers to climbing sideways, parallel to the ground, across a rock face.

Undercling – An upside-down handhold. The climber may use this hold by pulling upward on it or by grasping the hold in a palm-up position.

UIAA – Union Internationale des Associations d'Alpinisme, an international organization that sets safety standards/guidelines and tests climbing safety equipment.

Whipper – Refers to taking a significant fall.

Understanding Climbing Communication

Climbing communication refers to standard phrases or words that allow the climbing team to communicate before, during, and after the climb.

To ensure safe climbing, communication between climbers is vital. This rule is especially true between climbers and belayers.

Miscommunication or a lack of attention results in accidents and occasionally a fatal event.

Climbers are expected to use the commands at all times to guarantee the safety of all climbers.

Belay Commands

"On Belay?" – This is a command from the climber to the belayer, given before the climber starts to ascend the route. It means, "Are you ready, do you have me on belay?"

"Belay on" – This is a command from the belayer to the climber, given before the climber starts to ascend the route. It means "I have you on belay, you are safe."

"Off belay" – This is a command from the climber to the belayer, given once the climber has descended and is safely on the ground. It means "I am safe, take me off belay."

"Belay off" – This is a command from the belayer to the climber, given once the climber has descended and is safely on the ground. It means "I understand you are safe; I am taking you off belay."

"Climbing" – This is a command from the climber to the belayer, given when the climber begins to climb. It means "I am climbing now."

"Climb on" – This is a command from the belayer to the climber, given when the climber begins to climb. It means "I am ready and alert, go ahead and climb."

Climbing Commands

"Slack" – This is a command from the climber to the belayer, given during a climb. It means "Do not hold the rope tight."

"Up rope" – This is a command from the climber to the belayer, given during a climb. It means "Pull slack out of the rope."

"Tension," "Take," or "Tight Rope" – This is a command from the climber to the belayer, given during a climb. It means "Pull the rope tight and hold me."

"Watch me!" – This is a command from the climber to the belayer, given during a climb. It means "Pay attention, I might fall."

"Falling!" - This is a command from the climber to the belayer, given during a climb. It means "I'm falling, you need to lock off the rope and hold me with the belay."

Descent Commands

"Ready to lower" – This is a command from the climber to the belayer, given when the climber is ready to descend. It means "I am ready to lower down."

"Got you!" - This is a command from the belayer to the climber, given when the climber is ready to descend. It means " I feel your weight on the rope, and I am ready to lower on your command."

"Lowering" – This is a command from the belayer to the climber, given when the climber is ready to descend. It means "I am lowering you now."

"On rappel" – This is a command from the climber, given to anyone below. It means "Watch out; I am getting ready to rappel down."

"Off rappel" – This is a command from the climber, given to a partner above. It means "I have disengaged from the rappel ropes; you may rappel down now."

Using the Terms

While on paper, these commands may seem confusing, but in practice, they are quite easy to use.

For example:

    Climber: "On belay?"

    Belayer: "Belay on."

    Climber: "Climbing."

    Belayer: "Climb on."

    Climber: "Take tension."

    Belayer: "Tension on."

    Climber: "Ready to lower."

Belayer: "Got you!"

Climber: "Lower."

Belayer: "Lowering."

Climber: "Off belay."

Belayer: "Belay off."

Be sure to use any climbing commands you may need during the climb, such as "watch me," and especially "falling!"

Understanding Climbing Grades

Although climbing grades tend to be subjective, you will need a basic understanding of grades and what they mean.

Climbing grades indicate how easy, moderate, or severe a specific climbing route is. In terms of the different types of climbing, all grades are not created equal.

Climbing grades do not take into account how dangerous a course may be, only the physical difficulty of the climb. It is important to note that difficulty may vary by the location of the climb.

Grading a Climb

In America, the climbing grades system is based on the Yosemite Decimal System (YDS). The YDS ranges from class 1, which is hiking, to class

5, which is technical rock climbing.

Technical rock climbing includes top-roping, sport climbing, and traditional climbing.

Class 5 is further broken down into difficulty grades from 5.0 to 5.15, with 5.15 currently representing the highest climbing grade in the world.

* * * * * * * *

In general, for technical climbing, the breakdown is:

- 5.0 to 5.7 is considered easy

- 5.8 to 5.10 intermediate

- 5.11 to 5.12 hard

- 5.13 to 5.15 extremely challenging

Grading Systems for Bouldering

American bouldering is graded using a scale known as the Hueco System or the V-system. This system ranges from V0 to V16.

Beginners should start with V0, as this is considered easy, while V16 is for the more skilled climber. As with the Yosemite Decimal System, the V-system does not take into account the danger factor of a possible climb.

Conversion Chart

Yosemite Decimal	Hueco Scale
5.5	VB
5.6	VB
5.7	VB
5.8	V0
5.9	V0
5.10a	V0
5.10b	V1

5.10c	V1
5.10d	V2
5.11a	V2
5.11b	V3
5.11c	V3
5.11d	V4
5.12a	V4
5.12b	V5
5.12c	V5
5.12d	V6
5.13a	V6
5.13b	V7
5.13c	V8
5.13d	V9

Climbing Etiquette

Learning proper climbing etiquette is equally as important as learning the lingo.

Here are a few things to keep in mind:

Be aware of your surroundings – You should always be mindful of where you are standing concerning other climbers. This rule is true of yourself as well as your belongings. If someone falls on you, it is your fault.

The person on the wall has the right-of-way – Before ascending a climb, always look first to make sure that your route does not interfere with another climber already on a route.

Brush it off – It is considered a common courtesy to brush holds that have accumulated excess chalk. Also, be mindful to not jump on a wall immediately after someone has cleaned it and is putting away the brush. Only jump on the wall if the person who brushed it does not intend to climb.

Do not offer unsolicited beta – Do not ruin a possible climb or problem on a bouldering wall by giving away the strategy. The fun is often in figuring out the route, so always ask first before offering suggestions or advice.

Take turns – Climbing gyms tend to be busy places, and while there is no limit to the time on the wall, it is vital to remember that others may be waiting to climb your route.

Clean up – This rule is critical if you are climbing outdoors. Respect nature by picking up any trash, whether it belongs to you or not. When climbing outdoors, always leave it better than you found it.

Learning the rules and terminology of climbing can seem like a daunting task, but do not be afraid to make mistakes.

Making mistakes is expected while learning the process. When in doubt, always be safe and always ask questions.

Gear Up

The beauty of being a new climber is that you can choose to own as much or as little gear as you like. You may even opt for no gear.

Renting equipment from an indoor gym can be a helpful way to familiarize yourself with different brands, types, and styles.

However, choosing the right gear for you ultimately depends on personal preference and safety.

Having the proper equipment is arguably one of the most vital factors when it comes to learning how to rock climb.

A climber puts a great deal of trust in their gear; therefore, you should always buy high-quality equipment meant exclusively for climbing.

For this book, we will only discuss the necessary equipment needed for bouldering and top-rope climbing.

Climbing such as sport and traditional, are considered more advanced.

To get you started bouldering or top-roping, you will need:

- Shoes
- Harness
- Chalk and chalk bag
- Belay device
- Carabiners

Shoes

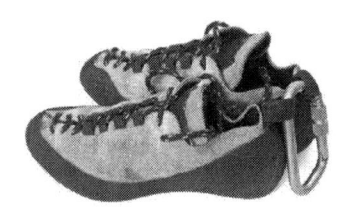

Shoes are often considered to be the most critical equipment a climber can buy.

Shoes are made up of a heel cup, the soles, the rand (the rubber that covers the toe), the upper, and the insole. Climbing shoes come in an assortment of styles, Velcro or lace-up, synthetic or leather uppers. The thickness of the rubber varies.

Although hundreds of climbing shoes are available, picking your first pair does not have to be complicated.

Selecting Shoes

Climbing shoes come in three main types:

- Neutral

- Moderate

- Aggressive

It is a common practice for climbing shoes to be worn a half size to two sizes down from your regular footwear. Such a large size-range makes it imperative to try on the shoes. Also, consider that new shoes stretch out after use.

When selecting a shoe, it should fit snugly, with no dead space around the foot.

A shoe that fits too big will cause the foot to slide around within the shoe, resulting in sloppy climbing.

Despite fitting snuggly, the shoes should still feel comfortable after several hours of wear.

> **For the novice climber, a neutral "all-around" shoe is preferable.**

All-around shoes are as they sound; they are versatile and are able to be used in many types of climbing. Whether climbing indoor, outdoor, on granite, or sandstone, an all-around rock climbing shoe will have you covered.

Proper Use of Shoes

Climbing shoes should come to feel like a second skin on your feet. Some climbers choose to wear socks with their shoes, while others prefer none for increased sensitivity. Whether you wear socks or not is simply a matter of preference.

A key point to remember is that climbing shoes are never to be worn for hiking or walking on a rough trail.

While it is fine to walk around an indoor gym, most outdoor terrain can quickly wear out your shoes when used for activities other than climbing.

It is common for a climber only to wear

shoes when they are ready to ascend.

Likewise, the belayer frequently wears regular shoes while belaying and then changes to climbing shoes when prepared to climb.

Also, take care to never walk around with only your toes slipped into the shoe, as this will quickly degrade the heel cup.

Caring for Your Shoes

Active climbers may go through as many as two pairs of shoes a year, while more avid climbers may go through three or more pairs. Buying shoes frequently can become pricey.

Adequate care of your shoes will go a long way in helping them last and perform longer.

Beware that climbing shoes worn without socks can lead to a nasty odor, and for this reason, it is essential to air your shoes out immediately after climbing.

Allowing your shoes to dry out will not only minimize odors but prevent the growth of bacteria and mildew. It may be beneficial to use deodorizing foot powder or sprays.

Never store shoes in direct sunlight or excessive heat. Heat can weaken the glue and cause the rubber to breakdown.

Always store shoes in a cool, dry place. After climbing, wipe the soles and rand lightly with a wet rag to remove excess dirt and then wipe dry thoroughly.

Dirty uppers can be spot-cleaned with rubbing alcohol or a small amount of water. If you have shoes with leather uppers, do not clean with excess water, as this can cause the leather to breakdown.

Safety Inspection

Be sure to inspect areas of high-wear on the soles and rands regularly. Keep an eye out for thin or pitted areas in the rubber.

Areas of high-wear include the toe area and

ball of the foot, as well as where the sole meets the rand. Always replace your climbing shoes or have them re-soled as soon as you find excessive wear and tear.

Dirty shoes or shoes with excessive wear will cause the climber to have less grip on the rock.

Harness

The climbing harness is another critical piece of equipment, and when chosen well, can provide years of climbing safety and comfort.

Like shoes, harnesses come in a variety of brands and styles.

- An "all-around" harness
- A gym harness
- Alpine and big wall harnesses

The standard climbing harness is made up of a waist belt and leg loops made of durable nylon webbing. It also includes safety buckles, a belay loop, gear loops, and two tie-in loops or hardpoints. Also, harnesses may be either padded or non-padded and specific to men or women.

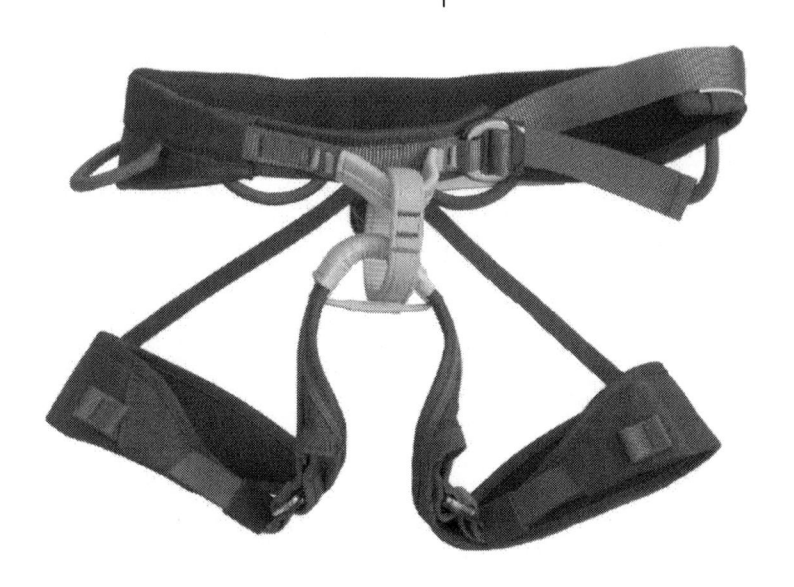

Selecting a Harness

Generally, the type of climbing will determine the proper harness. In the case of the new rock climber, an all-around harness is the harness of choice, as this is a traditional multipurpose harness.

These types of harnesses are almost always padded and feature an adjustable waist and leg loops for added comfort and a perfect fit. Finding a quality fit in a climbing harness is vital.

To fit a harness properly:

1. Begin with the waist and leg loops entirely loosened, if adjustable.

2. Step into the harness by stepping into the waist belt and leg loops, the same as you would step into pants. Situate the waist belt so that it sits above the hip bones and then securely tighten.

You should never be able to pull the harness below your hips. A harness that can be drawn below the hips may cause the climber to slip out easily. To ensure the waist belt is secure, you should have no more than a two-finger gap between your waist and the waist belt.

3. Finally, make sure to double back the buckle of the waist belt.

4. After securing the waist belt, adjust the leg loops one at a time. The placement of the leg loops is based more on comfort than safety. However, they should fit snugly around your legs.

The leg loops should not pinch, slip, or restrict the climber's movement. Leg loops that are snugger will allow you to feel comfortable while hanging freely in the harness. In contrast, looser leg loops are not as soft when hanging freely.

Without testing a harness, you cannot accurately tell if it will be comfortable or an accurate fit.

Most sports and recreation stores and indoor gyms will have a testing area to allow you to try the harness out.

To test a harness, sit in it, or put weight on it. The harness should not have obvious points of pressure, dig into you, or shift excessively.

A quality weighted harness will remain comfortable when sitting upright in it, similar to sitting in a chair.

Proper Use of a Harness

The harness utilizes the waist and leg loops to attach your body to the climbing rope. A figure-eight knot is tied in the climber's end of the line to connect the harness to the climbing system.

First, the tail of the figure-eight is passed through the leg hardpoint, located below the belay loop.

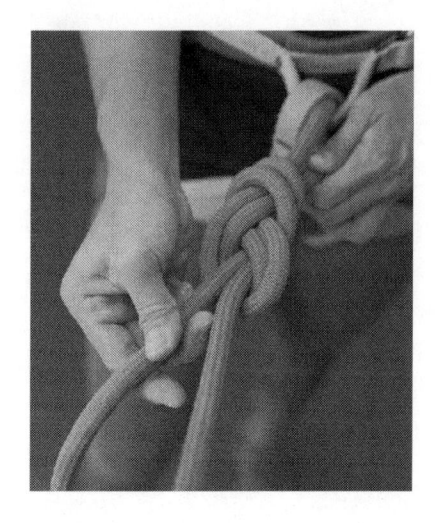

63

Next, the same tail end is passed through the waist hardpoint, situated above the belay loop. Finally, the tail end of the rope is traced back through the figure-eight in the line, creating a secure figure-eight knot.

The belay loop on the harness connects the waist belt and leg loops.

Belay loops are attached to a belay device via a locking carabiner.

The belay loop is also the point of attachment for the carabiner in an auto-belay system.

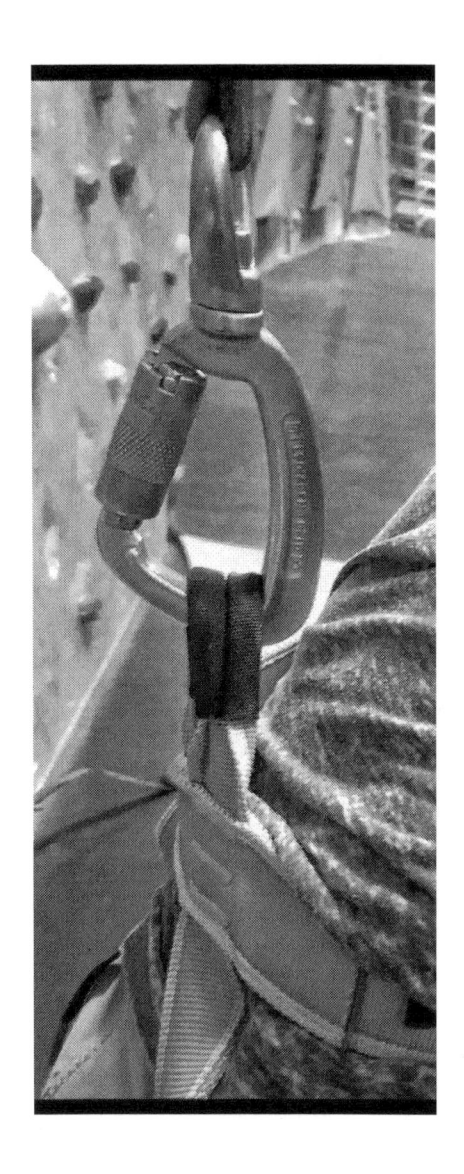

To the rookie climber, this exercise of using a harness may sound puzzling.

However, there is plenty of guidance and practice tying-in in an introductory climbing class provided by a climbing gym or sports and recreation store.

Caring for a Harness

Depending on how frequently and the conditions in which you climb, the nylon webbing will degrade and weaken over time.

With proper care and maintenance, a standard climbing harness can last roughly three years.

This lifespan may be reduced or extended depending on how well the harness is maintained.

A climbing harness should be stored in a dark, dry location, away from sharp objects.

Take care to keep the harness away from gasoline and other corrosive substances such as bleach, solvents, or battery acid.

Corrosive substances can quickly degrade the life of the harness.

Ideal storage should be out of direct sunlight

and excessive heat, preferably in a harness bag.

For a dirty harness, rinse it with water.

If rinsing fails to remove dust and debris, you may gently hand wash the harness.

Take care to only use warm water and mild soap and never use bleach.

After being hand-washed, the harness should be rinsed and hung to drip-dry, away from direct sunlight.

Safety Inspection

Regular climbing will wear a harness out, and repeated strenuous falls can weaken tie-in points.

To ensure maximum safety, you should make it a habit to inspect the harness for signs of damage before and after each trip to the crag. Inspect the harness for things such as frays, tears, rips, holes, or abrasion in the webbing.

Look for buckles that are cracked or damaged in any way. Be mindful of any faded areas, as this means the webbing has faded due to sun exposure.

Any harness involved in a severe fall should be retired immediately, even if there is no visible damage. Likewise, if you have any doubts about the reliability of your harness, retire it immediately.

It is considered good practice to destroy any gear that you have doubts about to prevent possible use by others.

Chalk and Chalk Bag

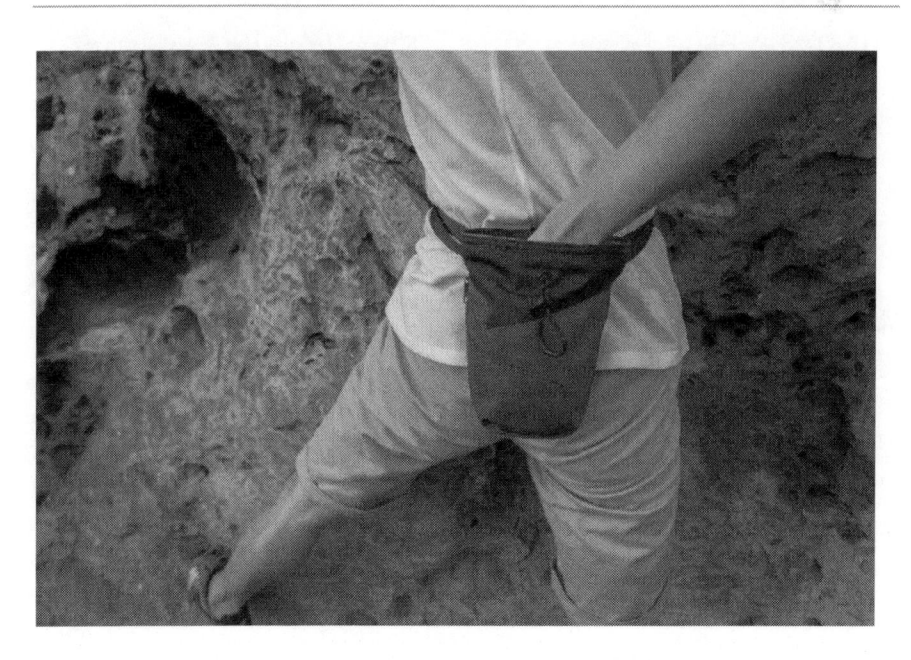

As a climber, you will find that your hands are prone to sweating under certain conditions. Your hands will sweat when the weather is hot and humid, and when you are new to climbing, your palms get sweaty when the route is scary.

As you can imagine, wet hands make for a terrible grip on the rock.

For this reason, climbers use chalks to absorb moisture and keep their hands dry.

As straightforward as chalk and bags are, there are still several options available for both.

Types of chalk include:

- Loose
- Block
- Liquid
- Eco chalk

Bags include small and standard size bags and chalk buckets.

Even with minimal considerations, the type that you pick is entirely personal preference.

Selecting Chalk

Over-analysis when selecting chalk and a bag is not necessary.

> *It is okay to pick chalk based on how it feels and which form you prefer.*

Types of chalk include:

Loose chalk – Loose chalk is chalk that is ground up and placed in a bag or bucket. It may come as pure chalk or chalk that contains drying agents.

Chalk balls – Chalk balls are porous sacks designed to hold the chalk and keep it from spilling. Place the chalk ball in your bag and rub it on your hands as needed.

Block chalk – Block chalk is chalk in a substantial chunk, requiring crushing. Block chalk can be crushed to the desired consistency and is less messy to transport before being broken.

Liquid chalk – Liquid chalk is a chalk-alcohol blend for rubbing on the hands. Once the alcohol dries, a chalk residue forms on the hands. This type of chalk is less messy and reduces marks on the rock.

Colored chalk – Colored chalk is chalk that matches the color of the rock for less of a visual impact. Many non-climbers do not view a chalk-covered crag as attractive. Likewise, a build-up of chalk creates a slippery surface for the climber.

Eco chalk – Developed in response to concerns over the dirtying of rock surfaces, eco chalk uses a colorless drying agent.

Selecting a Chalk Bag

There are no frills here. A chalk bag is simply a reservoir to hold loose chalk or chalk balls.

Packs consist of a strap worn around the waist.

Another option for wear is clipping it to the waist belt of the harness.

Bags come in small sizes, meant for those with little hands, and standard sizes.

Buckets are not intended to be carried by the climber but instead sit on the ground.

Buckets for dipping the hands into are ideal for groups of boulderers.

Optional bag features include:

Cord closure – The cord closure prevents chalk from spilling out of the bag.

Fleece lining – The fleece lining helps to hold down the chalk dust. It also aids in evenly distributing the chalk on your hands.

Stiff rim – The thick lip on the bag helps to hold the bag open. It allows the climber's hand to slip in and out quickly.

Zippered pocket – Some bags feature a zippered pocket for holding items like keys or lip balm.

Brush loop – This feature holds a brush, which allows the climber to clean chalk off of holds easily.

Proper Use of Chalk and Bag

Unless you are using liquid chalk, other types of chalk may be placed in a bag and used as needed.

Apply the chalk by dipping your hands into the bag one at a time.

Spread the chalk over your palms and fingertips. Allow the excess chalk to pour back into the bag.

Blow away any loose particles, so a smooth chalk layer covers your hand.

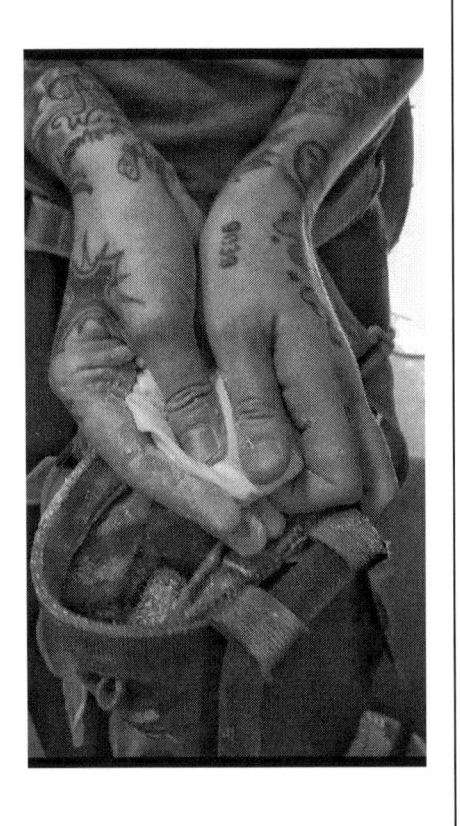

When using chalk, it is considered good practice to leave no chalk trace behind.

Leaving chalk smears and tick marks are poor etiquette.

When climbing outdoors, use chalk sparingly and always carry a brush to remove any excess.

Always ask about the use of chalk, as some climbing areas prohibit it altogether.

Hand Care

Chalk helps the climber hang on longer, but it is also tough on the skin. Having a hand care routine is imperative.

Always wash your hands with soap and cold water after climbing, which will help with callus management.

Keep in mind blisters will be inevitable as a new climber.

Here are some tips to try for healthy hand management:

Nail Clipping – Nails should preferably be clipped and maintained before climbing.

Filing – Using a file or sanding block on the hands, as well as the nails, will help to file down any nicks or rough spots. Filing helps to prevent skin from catching on holds and ripping open.

Hand salve – A nourishing hand salve will keep your hands moist and elastic while helping to prevent cracks.

Athletic tape – Athletic tape may be used to protect the fingers, wrist, and hand and provides extra support.

Belay Device

A belay device is designed to let the belayer control the rope by applying friction and drag to it.

The tool, as well as the belayer's brake hand, helps maintain tension on the line to hold, lower, and catch the climber in a fall.

Another use of the belay device is rappelling, making this device a crucial tool for safe climbing.

When selecting a belay device, there are three types:

- Tubular
- Figure-eight
- Assisted braking

Most devices have two holes for the rope to make it easy for left or right-handed people.

Although the model you choose will depend on the type of climbing you do, the tubular belay device is the most popular and widely used.

Selecting a Belay Device

Not only are tubular belay devices popular, but it is most likely the device you will be trained to use in an introductory climbing class.

Tubular devices are best for the indoor gym, sport, and multi-pitch traditional climbing.

They are generally light, compact, and easy to use.

They accommodate a range of rope diameters and prevent the rope from twisting or kinking.

Tubular devices can also be used for rappelling, although some climber's find this application to be too slow.

Figure-eight belay devices are used primarily for rappelling as well as caving and search and rescue.

They may be fashioned to belay a leader or top-rope climber, but you are not likely to see this device in an indoor climbing gym.

They dissipate the heat caused by friction efficiently and work with almost any rope diameter.

One drawback is that it puts a twist in the climbing rope, making handling more difficult.

They also require more attention from the belayer and more force from the brake hand when compared to other devices.

Assisted braking belay devices are best for the gym, sport, and multi-pitch traditional climbing.

They are also called self-locking or auto-locking devices.

These devices are designed to lock down on the rope when a sudden force is applied, allowing the belayer to catch and hold a fall.

Assisted devices generally feed the line smoothly, but may not work with all rope diameters.

Although they may seem more convenient, these devices can be bulky and are often not allowed in climbing gyms.

Proper Use of a Belay Device

As a rookie climber, it is not likely that you will immediately learn to use a figure-eight or assisted braking belay device. These types of devices are considered more advanced and require expert training.

For this instruction, we will focus solely on the tubular style belay device.

When setting up a belay device, the rope is folded and pushed through one side.

The device and rope are clipped with a locking carabiner to the belay loop on the belayer's climbing harness or an anchor.

The friction caused by the rope's contact with the belay device slows the cable to protect the climber.

Do not worry if this information feels hard to grasp.

You will receive plenty of guidance and practice with connecting a belay device to the climbing system and belaying for a climber in an introductory climbing class.

Caring for a Belay Device

There is not much maintenance needed for a belay device, considering its heavy use.

Belay devices are generally reliable, as they are made from heavy aluminum or alloy.

Never leave your belay device near anything that could be potentially corrosive or reduce its lifespan.

Use your best judgment to protect your devices as you would protect any of your climbing gear.

Safety Inspection

Inspect belay devices for corrosion, cracks, and sharp edges regularly.

Check for excessive wear and any loose, bent, or missing pieces.

If you have any doubt regarding the safety and reliability of the belay device, retire it immediately.

Carabiners

The carabiner serves many roles in climbing.

It is essential for linking equipment into a safety system.

It consists of a frame and a spring-loaded gate that opens for attachment.

Carabiners come in different shapes, such as:

- D
- Asymmetric D
- Pear
- Oval-shaped

They also feature different gate styles like:

- Straight
- Bent
- Wire
- Locking gates

Carabiners are durable, lightweight, and made from aluminum or steel.

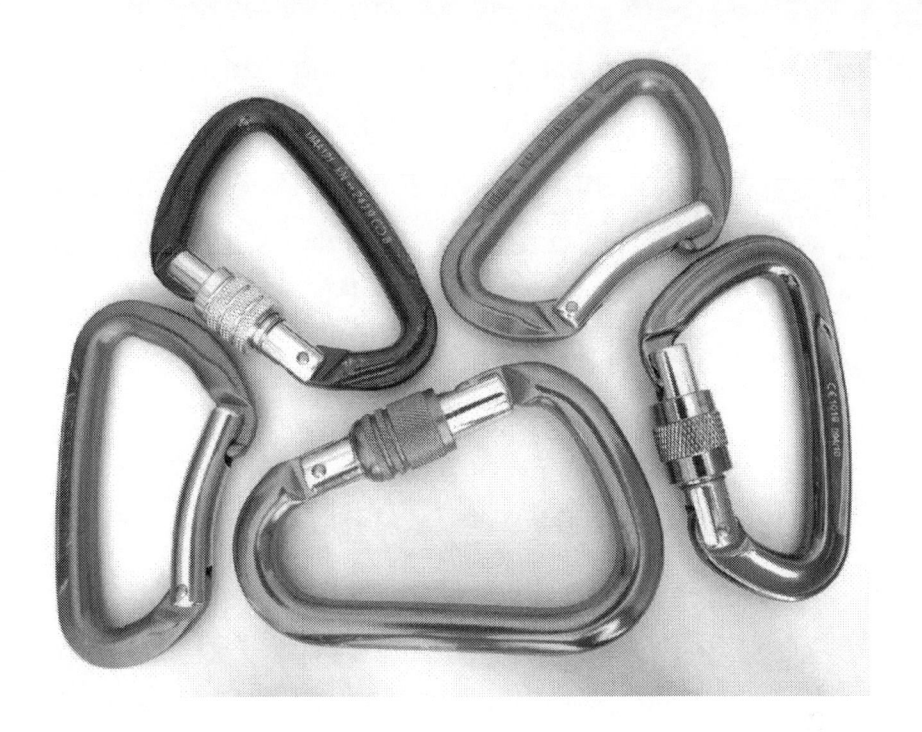

Selecting Carabiners

Different climbing tasks call for specific types of carabiners. Therefore, when choosing a carabiner, you should consider the shape, the gate type, the size, strength, and weight.

Here is a breakdown of carabiner shapes:

D – The D-shaped carabiner is considered to be the most robust shape and ideal for most types of climbing. It concentrates the force on the carabiner's spine, allowing for increased strength. It has a larger gate opening than an oval shape, but a smaller gate opening than the asymmetric D shape.

Asymmetric D – Asymmetric D is considered to be the most popular design of carabiners. This type of carabiner works like the regular D-shape, with the load put on the spine, but they have a narrow top end. This smaller end helps to reduce weight further. Asymmetric D-shaped carabiners are lightweight and robust and have large gate openings.

Pear – Pear-shaped carabiners are used mostly for belaying and rappelling. They have large gate openings for easy clipping but are more substantial than most other shapes. A standard pear-shaped, locking carabiner is preferable if you are unsure of what style you need.

Oval - Oval carabiners are ideal because the uniform curves limit load-shifting. Some drawbacks are that they are heavier and have a smaller gate opening.

Once you have a basic understanding of shapes, consider gate styles. Here is a breakdown of carabiner gate types:

Straight – Carabiners with straight gates have a variety of uses and are the most common. They are durable and easy to use and can be found on quickdraws or for racking gear. Straight-gate carabiners are less likely to come unclipped.

Bent – Bent-gate carabiners have a curved gate which makes clipping rope fast and easy. They are typically used in sport climbing for the rope-end of quickdraws.

Wire – Wire-gate carabiners utilize a loop of steel for the gate. This style allows for a full gate opening. They are ideal for climbing in wet, cold weather because they are less likely to freeze shut or to open in a fall than other types of gates.

Locking – Locking-gate carabiners, as the name implies, have gates that lock closed. They may be either screw-locking or auto-locking. Auto-locking gates automatically lock when the gate closes, while screw-lock gates are locked by turning the attached sleeve. Locking carabiners are the gold standard for use with belay and rappelling devices, as the locking gate adds security.

Proper Use of Carabiners

For top-rope climbing, the carabiner is used for belaying a climber.

The carabiner attaches to the belay loop of the harness.

The carabiner must pass through both the belay device and the rope, before being attached to the belay loop.

Always ensure the carabiner remains locked for added safety.

Caring for Carabiners

Fortunately, carabiners require very little maintenance. Always keep carabiners away from excessive heat.

Dirty carabiners can be washed in warm water and thoroughly dried before storage.

It may be helpful to spray the gates with a

lubricant occasionally, but any excess must be wiped off.

Use your best judgment to protect your carabiners as you would protect any of your climbing gear.

Safety Inspection

Regularly inspect the carabiner for excessive wear and any loose, missing, or faulty parts. Check for corrosion, cracks, and sharp edges.

Never drop a carabiner, as this can cause damage on impact. The gate and locking mechanisms should operate with ease, and locking sleeves should remain in a closed position.

Never leave your carabiner near anything that could be potentially corrosive or reduce its lifespan.

If you doubt the safety and reliability of the carabiner, retire it immediately.

Helmet

If you are learning to climb outdoors, you may also want to consider purchasing a helmet, rope, and crash pads. Also, you may need to consider items for creating anchors, which are discussed in a later chapter.

To ensure maximum safety, you should always climb with a helmet while climbing outdoors. Helmets protect against falling rocks and dropped equipment and prevent head injuries by absorbing energy under the impact.

When choosing a helmet, you should consider the type, fit, and the style of climbing you do.

Selecting a Helmet

There are two main types of climbing helmets, hardshell and shelled foam helmets.

Hardshell helmets may also be called suspension or hybrid.

Hybrid helmets are the most common type and consist of an outer hard plastic shell and an inner suspension system.

The internal suspension system allows the helmet to float on the head.

Hardshell helmets are inexpensive and have a long life lifespan.

Shelled foam helmets are lightweight and sit directly on the head.

They consist of a thick layer of foam for absorbing impact shock. They are less durable than a hardshell helmet, making them ideal for a climbing gym if a helmet is required.

Trying on different styles is the best way to determine if the helmet properly fits.

The helmet should remain secure and snug when you shake or tilt your head from side to side, forward and backward.

Adjust any buckles or chin straps so that there is no slack.

Proper Use of Helmets

Helmets should fit securely on the head and cover both sides, as well as front and back of the head.

Always inspect the helmet before putting it on and always read the manufacturer's instructions for use.

Caring for Helmets

Proper care and maintenance will prolong the life of the helmet. Helmets may be cleaned using a cloth and rubbing alcohol.

If you sweat a lot, it is best to wear a bandana. However, if the inside of the helmet requires

washing, hand wash in lukewarm water using a mild detergent. Ensure that you protect the helmet from chemicals and any corrosive substances.

Avoid putting stickers on your helmet, as the

solvents in the adhesive can damage the shell.

Do not expose the helmet to excessive heat or cold. Do not sit on or exert unnecessary pressure on the helmet. Do not use the helmet for any activities other than climbing.

Safety Inspection

Inspect your helmet before each use. Note the condition of the shell and foam liners. The foam should not be damaged or loose.

Look for any noticeable damage to the outer shell, such as significant dents. Check for any faulty buckles and hardware and any frayed or torn webbing.

Any helmet that is involved in a severe blow should be retired immediately, even if there is no visible damage.

Climbing Rope

The climbing rope is considered your lifeline. The cable consists of a braided sheath and core and comes in a variety of lengths, diameters, and types.

When selecting climbing ropes, you will need to consider type, features, diameter, length, and safety features.

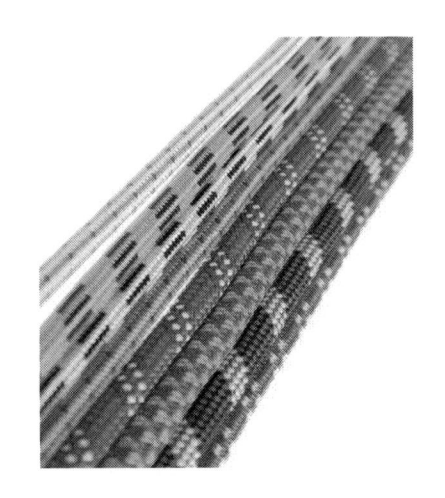

Selecting Rope

There are two basic types of rope: dynamic and static.

The dynamic rope stretches to absorb the forces of a fall, lessening the impact on the climber.

Static ropes do not stretch, making them more durable than the dynamic.

Static ropes are used mostly for rappelling, gear hauling, caving, and rescue work.

Static ropes should never be used to lead climb because they will not absorb impact in the event of a fall.

Dynamic rope is further broken down into three categories:

- Half
- Single
- Twin

Half – Half ropes are used for traditional, mountaineering, and ice climbing. A circled ½ symbol designates each end of the rope. Half ropes utilize two lines. One is clipped to protection on the left, and the other is clipped to protection on the right, allowing the rope to run straight and parallel. The half-rope technique reduces rope drag, but also requires expert skill and training, as it is more rope to manage.

Single – Single ropes are best used for top-roping, sport, traditional, and big wall climbing. A circled 1 symbol designates each end of the rope. Single lines are suitable for many types of climbing because they come in a variety of lengths and diameters.

Twin – Twin ropes are best used for traditional climbing, mountaineering, and ice climbing. A circled infinity symbol designates each end of the rope. Similar to the half-rope system, twin ropes use two lines. The difference in this system is that both strands are clipped through the same protection. Although it causes more rope drag, this system allows for faster rappelling than a single rope.

When considering rope diameter, a skinny rope is usually lighter but less durable. Thicker lines are more durable and abrasion-resistant. A thinner cable is preferable if you are hiking long distances to the crag, while thicker rope is better for the local peak.

Here is an overview of climbing rope diameter:

Single up to 9.4mm – These ropes are lightweight but less durable and harder to handle. A thin line tends to move rapidly through a belay device, requiring an experienced belayer.

Single 9.5 to 9.9mm – This diameter range is ideal for all-around use. Single ropes in this range are light, durable, and easy to handle.

Single 10mm and above – This diameter range is best used for top-roping and gym climbing, as well as navigating sport routes and big wall climbing. They are thicker and more durable.

Half and twin – Half ropes range from 8 to 9mm, while twin ropes are 7 to 8mm thick.

Static – Static rope diameter ranges from 9 to 13mm. They are frequently measured in inches; therefore, it is not uncommon to see a 7/16" diameter.

If you intend to climb outdoors, choosing the correct rope length is imperative. The dynamic rope ranges from 30m to 80m.

Generally, a 60m line is adequate in most situations. Be mindful that your rope must be long enough so that half its length is greater than or equal to the route you intend to climb.

To illustrate, if your route is 30m long, you will need at least 60m of rope to ensure there is enough rope to climb up and be lowered.

The following are standard rope features to look for:

Middle mark – A middle mark is included on most ropes. It is a mark, typically black dye, to help identify the middle of the cable.

Bicolor – Bicolor means that the rope has a weave pattern that differentiates two halves of the cable. It is often an easier-to-spot and more permanent middle mark than the traditional black dye middle mark.

Dry treatment – Ropes that include a dry treatment reduce water absorption. This feature is best for traditional, mountaineering, and ice climbing.

Rope consideration can be a lot of information for the novice climber.

When in doubt, a dynamic rope is standard for outdoor climbing.

An ideal rope for a beginner is a 10mm dynamic rope.

When in doubt, always seek the guidance of an expert when it comes to choosing rope.

Proper Use of Rope

Always use a rope bag that unfolds into a tarp, as it helps to protect your rope from dirt, dust, and damaging debris.

Do not ever step on the line, as this can grind

dirt into the sheath and core of the rope.

> **Ensure that the cable runs free and does not run over sharp edges that can cause cuts.**

It is good practice to keep a rope usage log that details:

- The frequency of use
- The number of significant falls
- Purchase date

Keeping a record helps to establish when it is time to retire the rope.

Caring for Rope

Clean your rope when it gets markedly dirty.

Rope wash is available at most retailers and allows you to wash the line in a machine, although a garden hose attachment works just as well. The rope should be thoroughly dry before climbing on it. Cleaning the cable extends the lifespan by keeping dirt off the sheath and core. Store coiled cables in a cool, dry location away from direct sunlight and any gasoline or petroleum-based products.

Safety Inspection

To fully know its condition, inspecting the climbing rope is vital before any climbing adventure.

To check your rope, thoroughly, run every inch of the line through your hands.

Look and feel for any damage that may include frays and fuzzy areas and any soft, mushy, or hard sections.

Note any areas of discoloration due to sun or chemical exposure.

Any rope that has endured a long fall should be retired immediately, even if there are no visible signs of damage.

Always purchase ropes that adhere to UIAA safety standards.

If you doubt the safety and reliability of the rope, retire it immediately.

Crash Pads

Outdoor bouldering requires crash pads to prevent injury in a fall. Crash pads come in different designs, sizes, and thicknesses.

Consider these options when selecting a pad. Also, consider portability, as bouldering requires the climber to carry the pad to the bouldering location.

Selecting Crash Pads

In terms of the folding design, there are different types of crash pads that include taco, hinge, and baffled designs.

Here is an overview of folding styles:

Taco – The taco design is a continuous piece of padding that folds in two, like a taco. Most taco crash pads come with backpack straps for portability. Taco pads are useful for laying directly over terrain to create a landing area. There are no hinges or openings for rocks to poke through, but they do not tend to lay flat and are not easy to store.

Hinge – The hinge design has a uniform crease through the middle, creating two sections of foam. Hinge-style pads often come with straps for portability. This type of design folds flat and is easier to store than the taco design. A drawback is that rocks can push through the hinged section, making them a poor choice for rough terrain.

Baffled – The baffled design consists of long tubes filled with foam and recycled material that are connected by partial hinges. Baffled crash pads lay flat on any terrain and fold securely but are denser than other pads. There is also the possibility of having more failure points due to having more hinges.

Crash pads come in two sizes: small and large, sometimes called medium and big or half and full.

The small pad is 3 feet by 4 feet, while the

large pad is 4 feet by 5 feet.

Small crash pads cover less landing area but are lighter and easier to transport and store.

Big crash pads cover more landing area but are more cumbersome and awkward to transport and store.

Different manufacturers use different types of foam based on type, composition, and thickness.

Foam options include open-cell, closed-cell, and memory foam.

Open-cell foam is soft and absorbent, and closed-cell foam is stiff and durable.

Memory foam is described as either soft or hard.

The composition of the pad depends on the number of layers used.

Generally, the thicker and stiffer foam pads can take significant falls and last longer but are too stiff for shorter falls.

The thickness ranges from 3.5 to 5 inches for a small and 4 to 5 inches for big pads.

Proper Use of Crash Pads

Crash pads must be placed thoughtfully to be effective. Consider the landing zone before climbing.

Decide on the fall trajectory and then put the pad in a fall zone that reduces the risk of injury. Crash pads can be used to cover boulders and fill holes between rocks.

Always have a spotter for safe climbing. While the climber ascends, the spotter can reposition the pads as necessary to reduce risk of injury.

Caring for Crash Pads

To extend the life of your crash pad, take care to brush off any dirt after climbing. Do not store in direct sunlight or excessive heat, as this will damage the foam and outer material.

Avoid dragging the crash pad across harsh terrain, instead, pick it up as much as possible. Any holes in the outer cover should be fixed right away to prevent damage to the foam.

Crash pads should not be stored while compressed or folded. Storing the pad in an open position will help to reduce wear and tear.

Safety Inspection

Inspect your crash pad before each use. Look for signs of excessive wear, holes in the outer cover, and discolored areas from sun exposure.

There should be no loose or exposed foam. As always, if you have any doubt about the safety and reliability of the crash pad, retire it immediately.

Climbing Clothing

When choosing climbing clothing, consider factors such as the environment, temperature, and weather.

Clothing for indoor climbing is mostly personal preference.

In general, the clothes you choose should move with your body without being restrictive. Shorts are an option for many climbers, but expose your legs to scraps and bruises from the rock or wall surface.

If you are climbing outdoors, always consider what clothing you will require for cold and warm weather climbs, as well as rain.

Concluding Advice about Equipment

Choosing personal climbing equipment can feel both exciting and overwhelming.

As a rule, most retailers do not accept returned equipment, so it is vital to be patient and pick quality equipment that is right for you.

As a beginner, try many types of gear and ask a lot of questions.

Your safety is your sole responsibility when you are climbing, and it is your responsibility to ensure that you have reliable gear.

Knots & Anchors

Knowing how to set up knots and anchors are vital skills necessary for the climber to utilize the system.

The safety of the climber is entirely dependent upon the strength and reliability of the knot and anchor.

For this reason, it is imperative to learn how to set up the system correctly.

This guide explains basic knots and anchors only.

Climbing Knots

In general, knots put the rope to work and help keep the climber safe. Knots are used for various tasks such as tying into anchors, tying into the rope, tying two ropes together, and for belaying, to name a few.

How well the knot is tied affects its strength;

therefore, it is essential to tie secure knots.

If the rope is the climber's lifeline, the knot is the life preserver.

While it is not necessary to learn every knot, knowing basic ones well ensures safe climbing.

To get started, here is an overview of knot terminology:

Knot – The term itself refers to a knot that is tied in a piece of webbing or rope.

Hitch – A hitch, while not technically a knot, connects a rope to other objects such as a carabiner or other ropes.

Working end – The working end of the rope refers to the end of the rope used to tie a knot.

Standing end – The standing end of the rope refers to the opposite of the working end. That is, the end of the rope not being used for knot tying.

Bight – The bight refers to a u-shape bend in the rope that does not cross itself.

Bend – The bend refers to a loop in the rope that crosses itself.

As a climber, thousands of knots can be useful, but knowing a few basic knots and hitches helps to complete an array of climbing tasks with ease.

If you have difficulty with knot-tying, there are several helpful online videos for reference.

For the rookie climber, this includes:

- Figure-eight follow-through
- Figure-eight on a bight
- Stopper knot
- Clove hitch

Figure-Eight Follow-Through

The figure-eight follow-through is arguably the most crucial knot, as it is used to tie the climber into the rope.

Also, it is used when setting up anchor points.

This type of knot is easy to tie and untie and easy to check.

The figure-eight is an excellent knot for strength and reliability, as the knot gets tighter when weighted.

To make a figure-eight follow-through knot, follow these steps:

1. Grasp the working (or tail) end of the rope with one hand and measure out a length of rope that extends from your hand to the opposite shoulder.

2. Create a bight from where you have measured at your shoulder. In many classes, this is referred to as creating a "ghost" or "alien." It is called so because the bight resembles a ghost or an alien head.

3. Wrap the tail end of the rope one full rotation around the bight, or "choke" the ghost or alien.

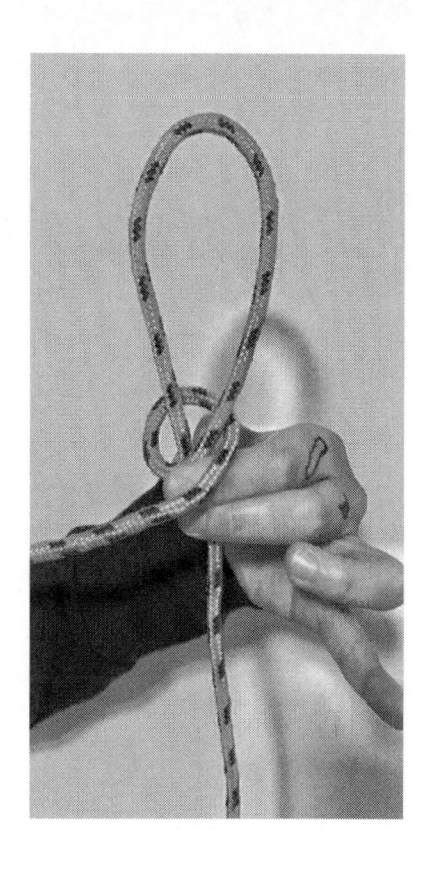

4. Put the tail end through the bight or loop, also known as poking the ghost or alien in the face.

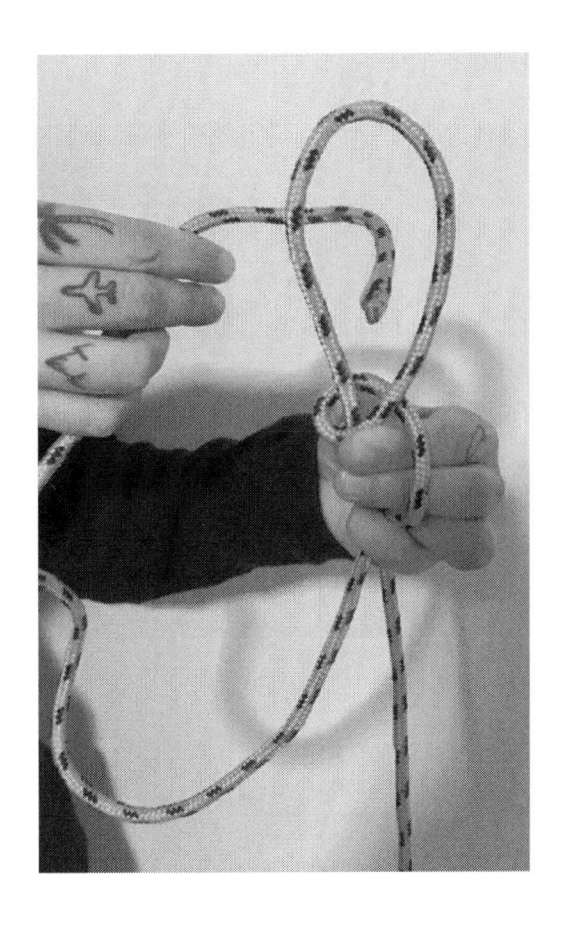

As you can see, this creates an "8" shape in the rope.

108

5. To tie into a harness and finish the knot, place the tail end through both hardpoints on the harness.

6. Then, use the tail to retrace the figure-eight in the rope.

7. To complete the knot, pull it tight to your waist and ensure that each line is parallel. There should be at least six inches of tail left.

To quickly check if the knot is correct, count five sets of parallel lines.

Figure-Eight on a Bight

The figure-eight on a bight knot is useful for anchor building. Just like the follow-through, it is durable, easy to use, and easy to check.

To make a figure-eight on a bight, follow these steps:

1. Make a bight in the section of rope you want to use and hold it in one hand.

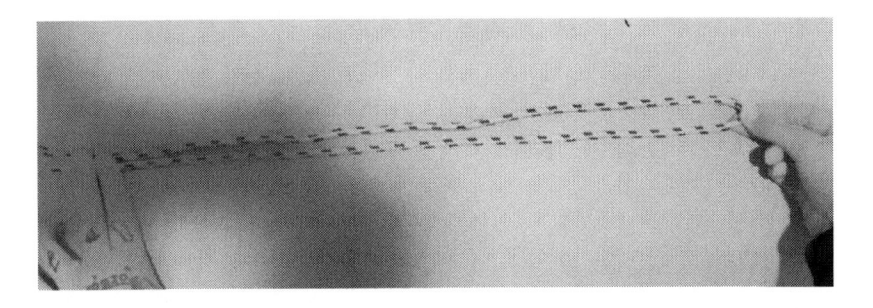

2. Cross the bight you are holding in your hand over the standing strands of the rope to form a loop.

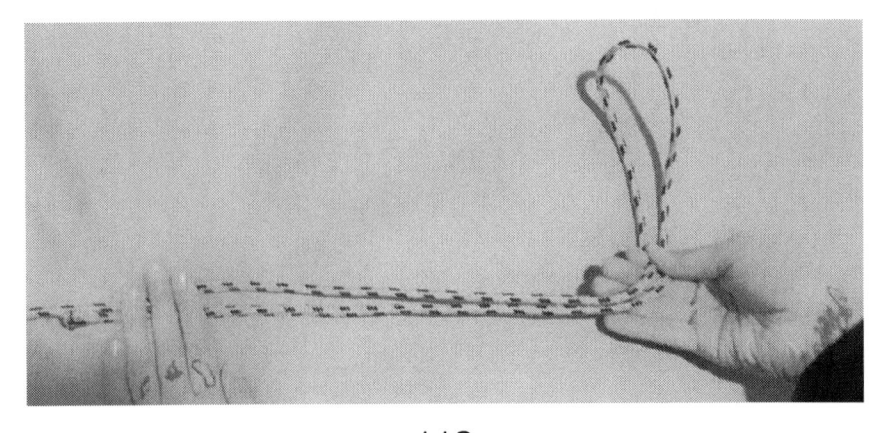

3. Bring the bight under the standing strands.

4. Pull the bight through the loop.

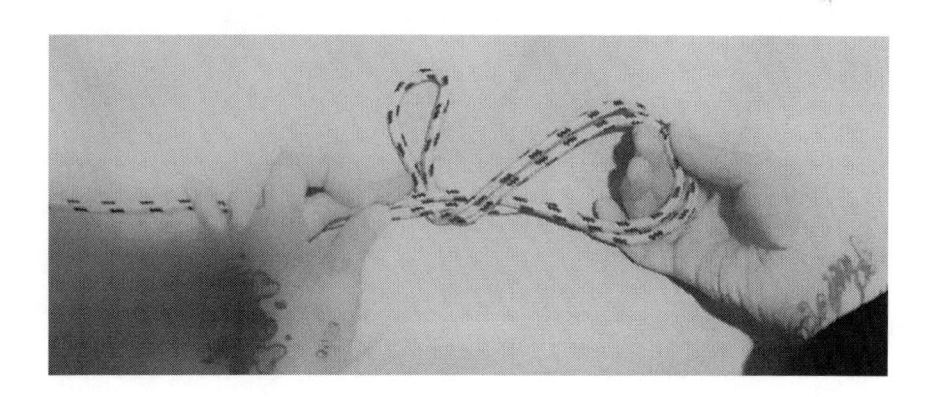

This figure-eight creates a loop at the end. To dress the knot, finish by pulling it tight.

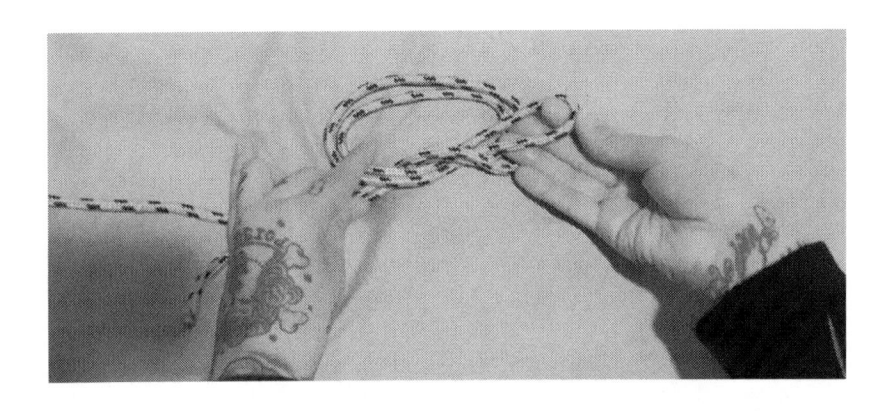

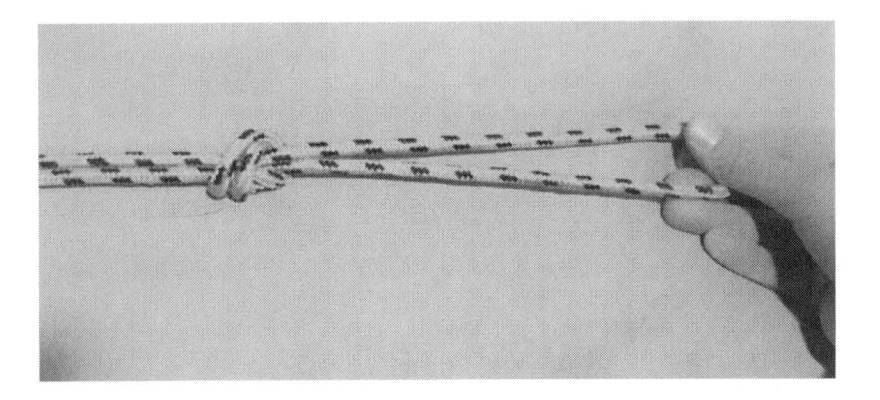

Stopper Knot

A stopper knot, also known as a double overhand, is a knot used to back-up other knots for safety.

Although the figure-eight is reliable, it never hurts to have a stopper knot for added security.

Be sure to tie the stopper knot as close to the knot you are backing up as possible.

To make a stopper knot, follow these steps:

1. Hold the knot you are backing up in one hand with your thumb against the rope.

2. Wrap the tail end fully over your thumb.

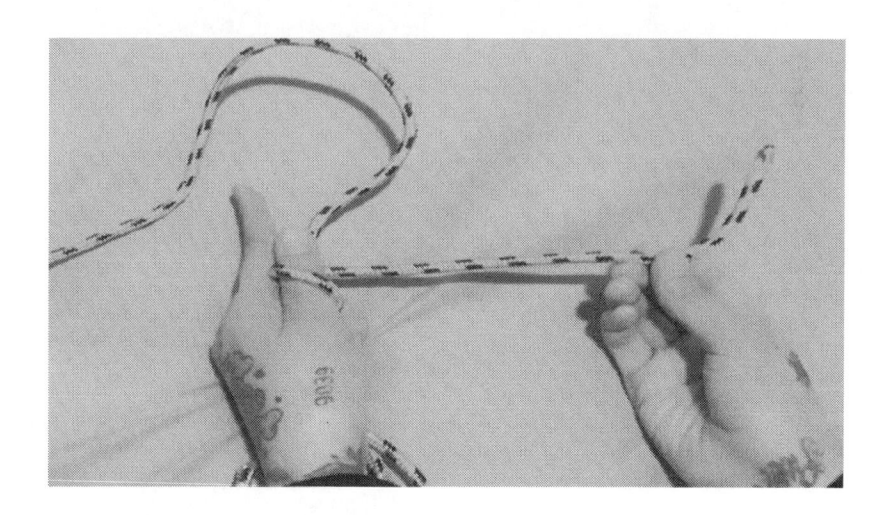

3. Fully wrap the tail end around again, going under the thumb, creating an X.

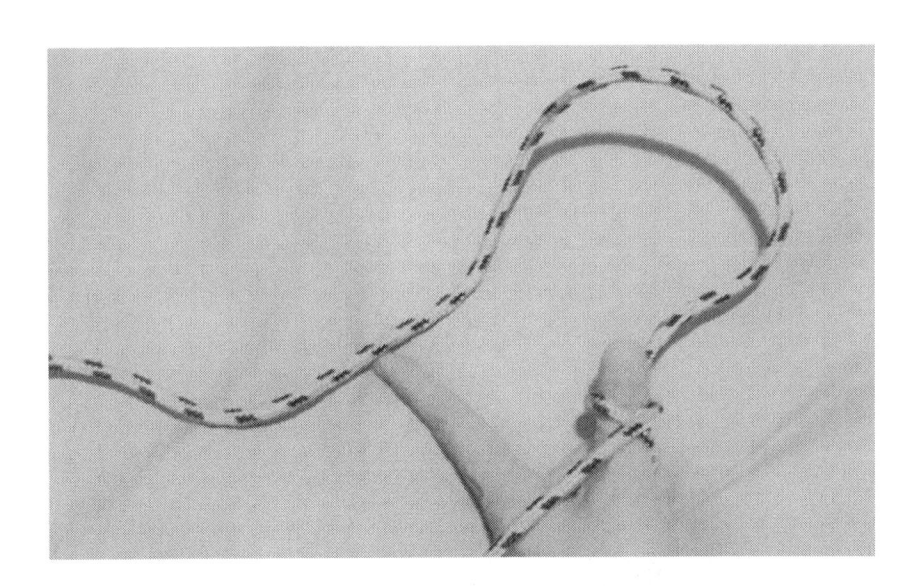

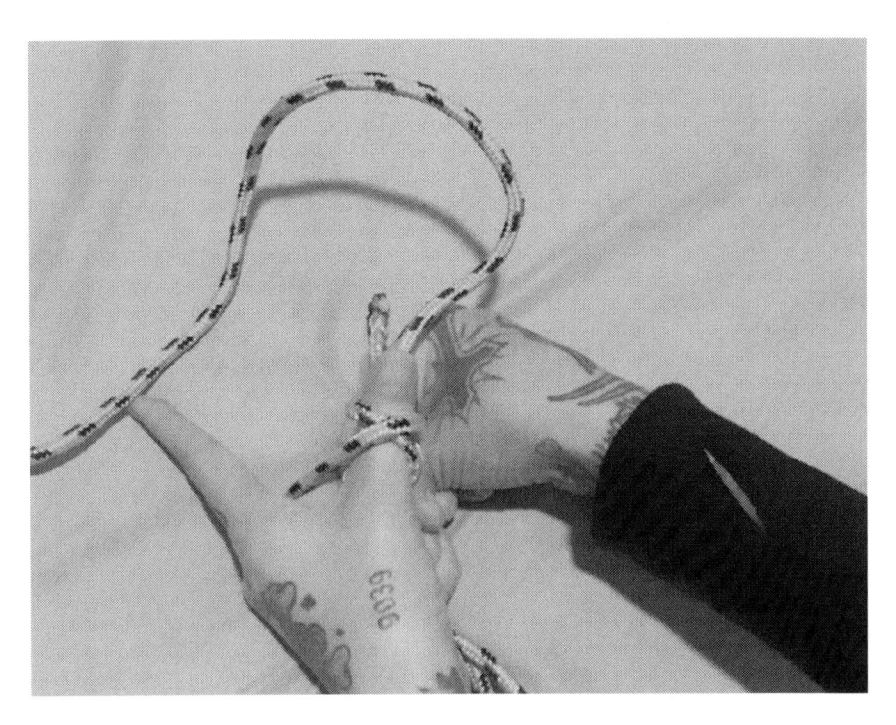

4. Slide your thumb out and push the tail through the formed X.

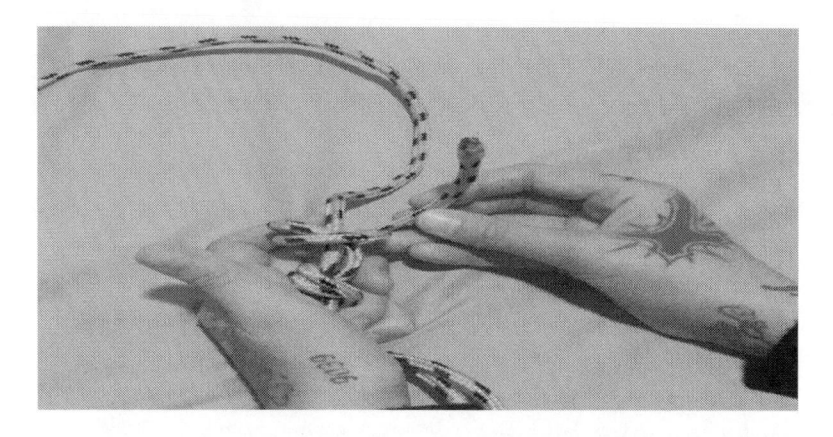

To dress the knot, finish by pulling it tight.

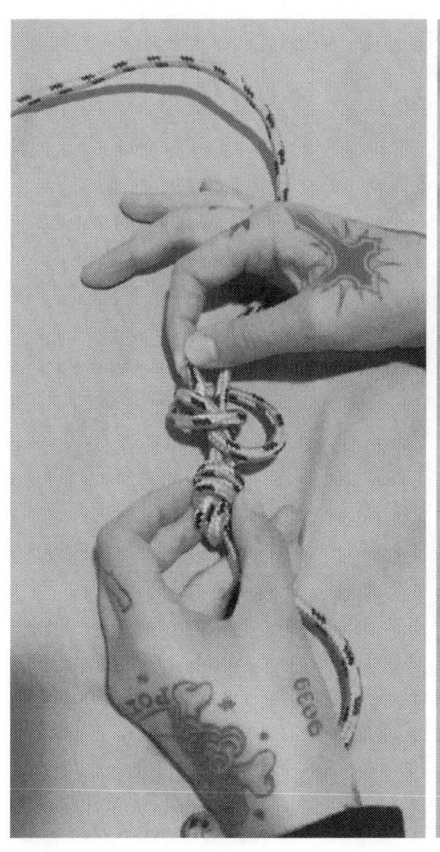

Clove Hitch

The clove hitch connects the rope to other objects like carabiners. It is useful for clipping yourself into anchors. It is easy to adjust and easy to tie and untie.

A clove hitch is typically tied onto a locking carabiner for safety.

To make a clove hitch, follow these steps:

1. Hold a section of the rope with two hands.

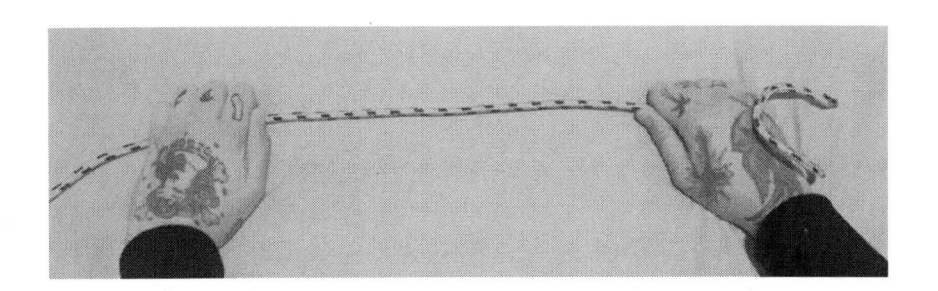

2. Form a loop by crossing the rope onto itself.

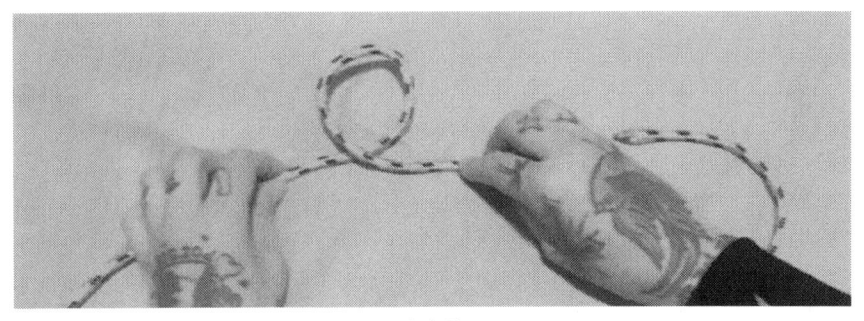

3. Form a second loop next to the first loop in the same manner.

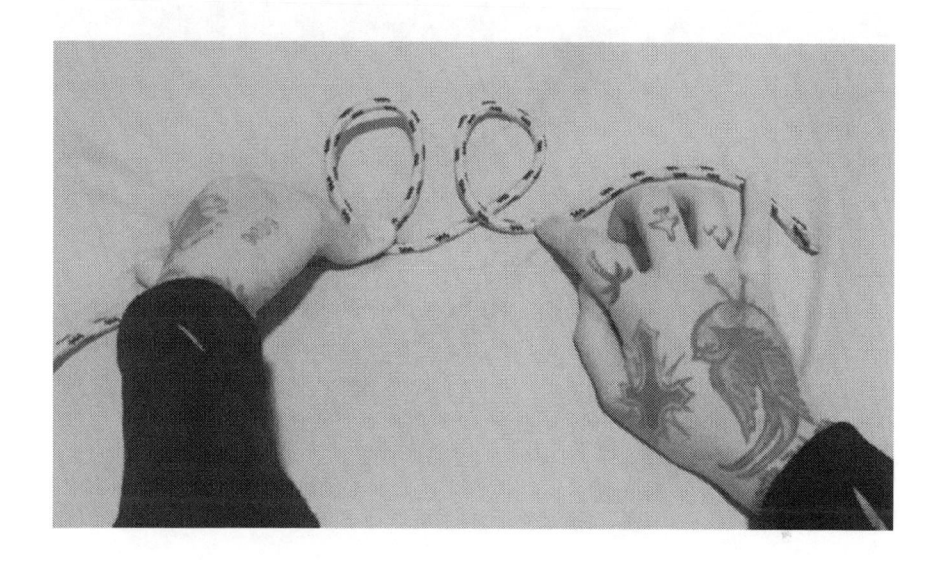

4. Place the second loop behind the first.

5. Clip both loops with a carabiner.

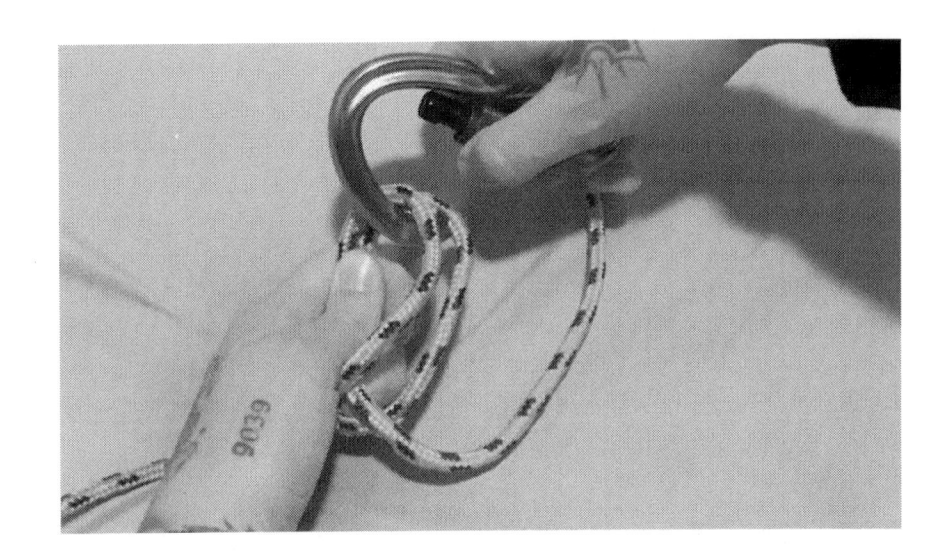

To dress the knot, finish by pulling each end tight on the carabiner.

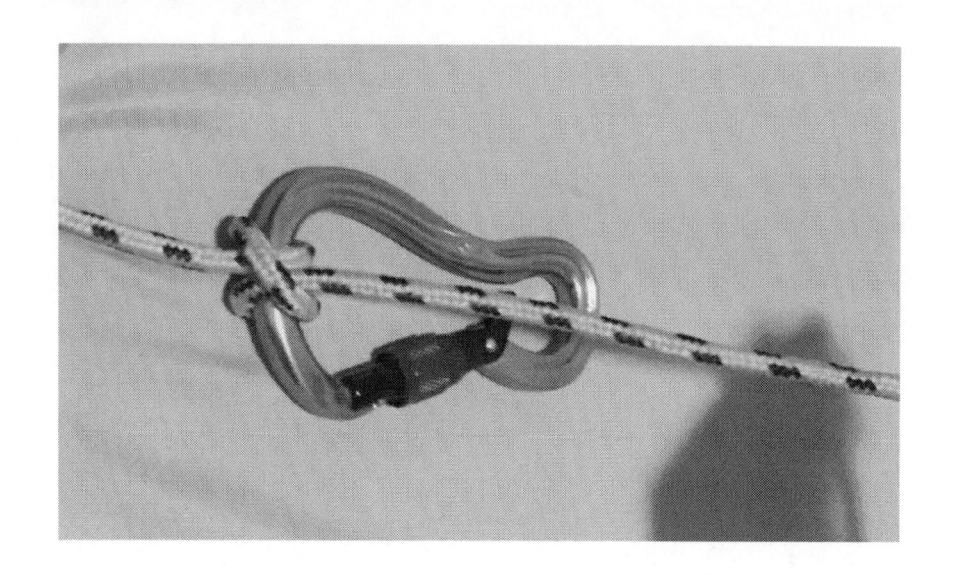

Climbing Knot Safety

Knots are essential for personal safety.

Tying a knot incorrectly or not finishing a knot could result in severe injury.

Practice tying knots over and over.

Always take your time and remember to complete your knot.

For added safety, double-check your knot and have a climbing partner double-check as well, your life depends on it.

Climbing Anchors

Commonly, climbing outdoors requires the climber to set up anchors.

The anchor system consists of individual anchor points that are connected to make a master point.

The climber attaches the rope to the master point to ensure safe climbing.

There are numerous anchor systems used in rock climbing and likewise, multiple ways of setting them up.

Anchor systems include:

- Natural anchors

- Fixed anchors

- Removable anchors

Setting up anchor systems, whether natural, fixed, or removable, is considered advanced for a new climber.

While this guide explains the differences between these anchors, it is not intended as an instructional how-to.

For personal safety, please always consult an experienced professional when learning to set up anchors.

Natural Anchors

Natural anchors are provided by the environment such as trees, boulders, and blocks of rock. These types of anchors are often more secure than gear that is placed for protection.

Slings and carabiners are all that are needed to create these anchors. When using natural features, always inspect them for strength and durability.

Trees should be alive, thick, and well-rooted in deep soil. When using rocks or boulders, ensure that they do not move. Check for signs of brittle rock areas that may suggest weakness.

Fixed Anchors

Fixed anchors refer to any hardware, usually bolts and pitons, that are placed permanently in the rock. These types of anchors are frequently two bolts fixed at the top of a climb. These fixed anchors may be accessed by walking or hiking to the top of the climb.

Quickdraws, single and double-length runners or slings, and cordelette may all be used when creating an anchor on two fixed bolts.

Anchors should be assessed for signs of weakness.

Check for excessive wear, cracks, and corrosion. Any bolt or piton that is moveable should not be used.

Removable Anchors

Removable anchors are placed when no natural or fixed anchors are available. Camming devices and nuts are used as removable anchors.

These items are securely placed in cracks of the rock. Advanced climbers with vast experience use this type of anchor system.

There are many things to take into consideration when setting up anchor systems, including direction, angle, and the forces applied to the anchor.

Every anchor you build is likely to be different each time. However, every anchor should be stable, redundant, and equalized every time.

An anchor that does not meet these criteria could mean life or death.

Although many acronyms for checking rope safety exist, the RENE system is simple and easy to follow:

R – *Redundant*. When building an anchor, redundancy is always necessary. Redundancy ensures that if one side fails, the anchor itself does not fail. A minimum of two anchor points should be used, although three are recommended. All parts of the anchor, including slings and carabiners, should display redundancy.

E – *Equalized*. Equalizing an anchor means that the load is distributed evenly between individual anchor points.

NE – *No Extension*. Anchors should be set up so that if one fails, it does not cause the master point to extend downward. The extension creates shock loading on the remaining anchor points, which, in turn, generates higher impact force.

You should double-check that <u>EVERY</u> anchor meets the RENE standard <u>EVERY</u> time. As your climbing career progresses, you will learn more knots and become more familiar with anchors.

Always master knots before attempting to learn to set up anchors.

As a reminder, your safety is your responsibility. Merely reading a climbing book or watching a video does not replace proper training or experience.

Always seek the help of an experienced, professional climber.

Climbing Technique

Anyone new to rock climbing is quick to notice a lot is going on during a climb.

The climber must consider where to place their hands and feet, how to position their body against the wall.

Climbers must determine the route of ascent, and no two climbers ever ascend the same way.

So much detail can leave the learning climber wondering how to make sense of it all.

To understand it requires working on technique.

While the technique may not come quickly to most people, in the case of rock climbing, technique refers to making the easiest possible movements, as smooth movements require less energy.

Technique consists of focusing on holds and body movement.

To further break it down, holds refer to how the rock is shaped and how to hold onto the shape. Movement refers to how to travel between the holds.

If you desire to become a better climber, working on technique is mandatory. While this is not a comprehensive list of holds or moves, it is a good starting point for practicing.

Handholds

Crimp – A crimp is a small edge that only fits the top pads of the fingers.

Jug – A jug is usually a hold broad and deep enough to fit your whole hand around.

Pinch – A pinch requires a squeezing action between the fingers and thumb.

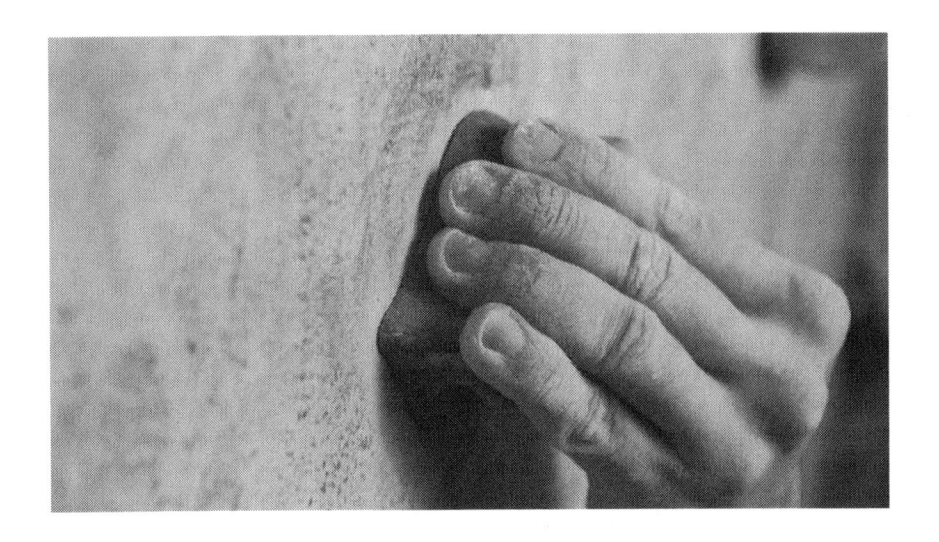

Pocket – A pocket is a section of rock that has a hole in it. Pockets can be deep or shallow, allowing the climber to place a whole hand in or just a few fingers.

Sidepull – A sidepull refers to any hold where the part your hand grabs onto faces sideways and away from you.

Gaston – A gaston is the opposite of a sidepull. The part your hand grabs onto faces sideways and towards you.

Sloper – Slopers are large, round holds and do not allow you to close your fingers around them, leaving your hand open.

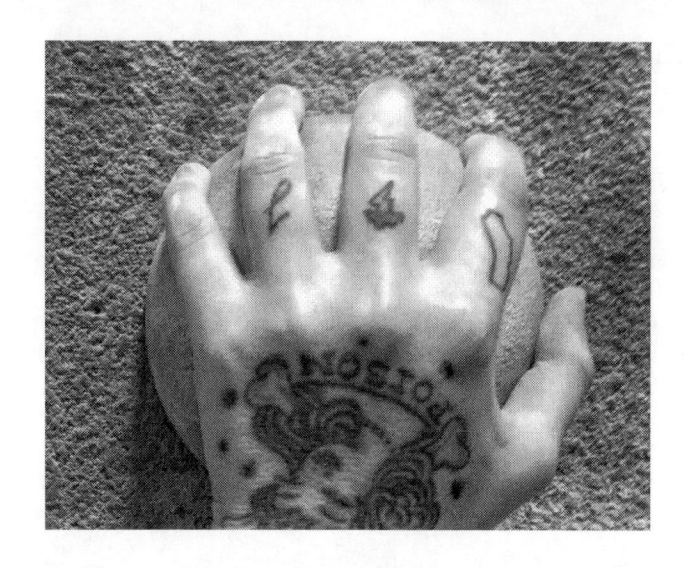

Undercling – On an undercling, the part of rock the hand grabs onto faces downward. An undercling becomes more comfortable to hold onto as you move your body above it.

Footholds

Edge – Edges use any part of the wall that sticks out enough to place the foot onto it. Edges mainly use the inside of the shoe and are essentially like walking upstairs.

Smearing – Smearing is used when there is no real foothold. When smearing, the sole of the shoe is pressed into the rock to create friction. Smearing is best for slabs and is similar to walking up a steep ramp.

Movements

Cross Through – It is logical to think the right-hand grabs hold only on the right side, and the left-hand grabs hold only on the left side. However, this way of thinking is not always efficient.

A cross through move allows the climber to reach across themselves to secure a hold. For example, if you have a secure grip in your right hand, but the next available hold is even further to the right, reach through and grab the next hold with your left hand.

Drop Knee – To do a drop knee, place your foot on a hold and then twist the knee down and towards the center of your body.

While it may sound complicated, dropping the knee allows the hip to rotate into the wall.

Twisting the hip into the wall naturally raises the arm on that side of the body allowing for a higher reach.

Flagging – Flagging refers to extending one leg out to press onto a blank part of the wall.

Flagging helps to lock the hip into the wall and maintain balance.

Match – Match refers to grabbing onto a hold with two hands.

Rock Over – A rock over is the act of moving your weight over onto a foothold.

This move is an essential climbing move and can be as tricky as placing your foot in line with your head.

In contrast, it may be as simple as a slight lean across.

The goal with the rock over is first to utilize sideways movement and then work upwards.

Last Words about Technique

The foundation of proper climbing technique is learning to use the lower body rather than using the arms to pull you upwards, which expends more energy.

In general, the arms should be kept as straight as possible while climbing and the hip close to the wall when possible.

Keeping your hip close to the wall also brings

your shoulder closer to the wall and helps maintain balance by keeping your weight over your feet.

__Use your eyes to look all around, and not just up, to spot secure holds.__

If you find yourself stuck, look for more footholds rather than handholds.

Regularly practicing useful techniques will help make you float up the wall you once found difficult.

Training to Climb

If you have not already learned, rock climbing is a demanding sport. It requires muscle strength, endurance, balance, and a certain degree of mental clarity.

Becoming a better climber is not solely about power and muscle; however, developing a training program can certainly help.

When starting, it is essential to set reasonable climbing goals and tailor your training to meet those goals.

Climbing uses several muscle groups from the feet and legs to the forearms and fingers.

While climbing is a great way to stay in shape, when overdone or done incorrectly, it poses the risk of severe injury.

For this reason, a focused training program will address these needs and help you realize your climbing potential.

Warming Up

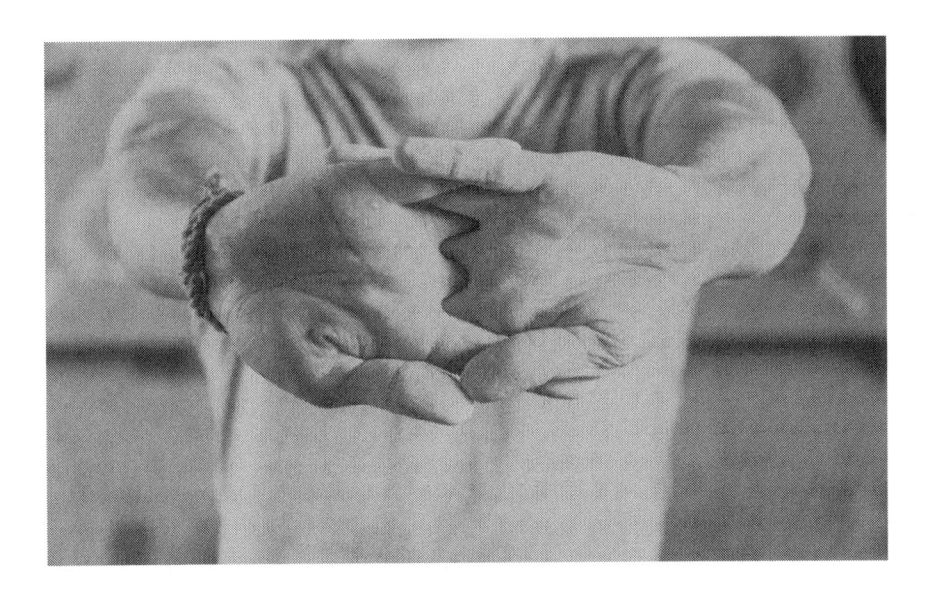

The importance of warming up cannot be overstated.

Climbing tends to put high forces on the tendons of the fingers and forearms.

Always start every training and climbing session with several minutes of stretching.

Stretching helps to loosen the muscles, which prevents injuries and makes the climber more limber overall.

Make sure to stretch the fingers, forearms, back and shoulders, and legs.

When preparing to climb, always do a

couple of easy routes before jumping onto a more challenging climb.

Warming up and stretching out allows the body time to get used to the range of movements necessary to ascend the wall.

Stretching should also be performed after a climb to allow the body to warm down.

Upper Body Training

A steep climb requires the use of the arms, shoulders, back, and core.

For the beginner who lacks overall fitness, simple pull-ups, push-ups, and sit-ups are an ideal place to start.

While sit-ups strengthen the core, pull and push-ups strengthen the chest, shoulder and back muscles and help to prevent shoulder injuries.

Incorporating internal and external shoulder rotation exercises also help to prevent injuries.

Weight training is another place to start, as it builds all-over body muscle.

When weight training, it is best to avoid heavy weights, which result in bulky muscles.

Bulky muscles tend to weigh a climber down.

To stay lean, combine high repetitions with light weights.

Hand Strengthening

There are not many other activities that require the finger and hand strength needed for rock climbing.

Hangboard training is a great way to build strength in the fingers, core, and upper body.

A hangboard is a tool that features different size grips that allow you to develop specific muscles by either hanging or pulling on various holds.

When learning to use a hangboard, starting with dead-hangs is recommended. To do a dead-hang, hang off the holds of your choice without pulling up or down.

Hang on for six to ten seconds and then let go. Rest for the same amount of time and then complete another set. Repeat this process three to five times.

While hanging, take care to engage your shoulder muscles by squeezing them together. Regularly performing dead-hangs builds tendon strength.

Once you feel yourself getting more comfortable and stronger with a dead-hang, move to pull-ups. To do a pull-up, select any two holds and do three pull-ups, rest and repeat.

Never do a pull-up on a hold you can barely grasp.

Be mindful of engaging your shoulders and your core.

To further engage your core, lift your knees to your stomach several times while hanging. Rest and repeat.

As you get stronger, attempt to hold your knees bent at the stomach for more extended periods.

Lower Body Training

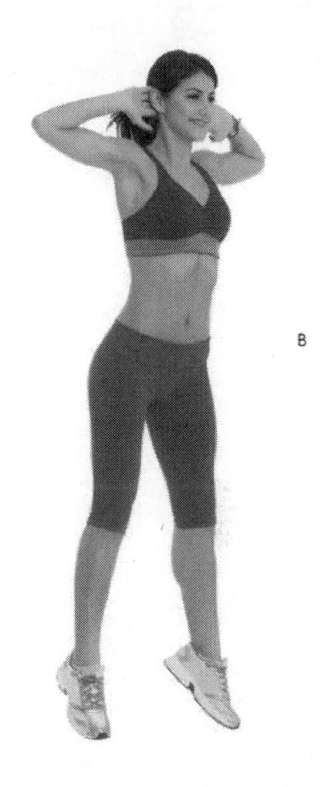

A   B

Leg strength is critical in climbing.

Proper climbing technique requires pushing your body up with your legs rather than using the arms to pull.

To build leg muscle, start with basic squats and lunges.

As you feel your legs grow stronger, advance to single-leg and jump squats.

Doing jump-squats conditions your legs for the frequent jumping off walls and landing that is involved in climbing.

Endurance

Endurance is needed to help the muscles be less fatigued and hang on for more extended periods.

This type of training enables you to climb continuously over longer periods or on longer routes.

Running, rowing, swimming, or biking, to name a few, are all excellent exercises for endurance.

Balance

When footholds are challenging, maintaining balance is a remarkable benefit.

Practicing yoga is an excellent way to develop balance. Other benefits of yoga include increased strength and flexibility. It is not uncommon for climbing gyms to offer yoga classes as well.

Getting Your Mind Right

Mental clarity is an aspect of climbing that should not be overlooked. Mental preparation is an excellent tool for a nervous climber.

To become mentally prepared, take a moment before each climb to visualize your route. Think about any worries you have regarding the climb and how you can prepare yourself to lessen those worries.

Take deep breaths and encourage yourself. Remind yourself to stay calm and believe in your abilities.

Fear of Falling

A fear of falling is often so frightening that it stunts a climber's growth. It is an instinct not to want to fall from a cliff, but this does not mean that you cannot safely fall in rock climbing.

One way to become more comfortable with falls is to take frequent falls while top-roping. Taking intentional falls conditions you to become comfortable with the sensation of the rope catching your weight.

Taking a fall also allows you to practice what to do while you are falling. Many climbing gyms and programs offer courses in how to fall correctly. Soon you may realize that the worst that happens is you go for a ride and have to start over.

A Note on Training

As you train to become a stronger, more efficient climber, it is crucial to take your time. Do not attempt what you are not ready for.

To avoid injuries, do not over-train and be sure to balance training time with gym time.

Be mindful of pain you may have while performing specific exercises.

If you have pain while performing any activity,

stop doing it immediately.

Tailor your training regimen to meet your climbing needs and goals.

You may find that planks are better for you than crunches, or that completing a bouldering problem builds better finger strength than hangboarding.

Work on areas of weakness, but keep in mind that physical training is not a replacement for proper technique or experience.

The only real way to become a better climber is to climb.

Climbing Safety

There is no doubt the sport of rock climbing is dangerous; however, that does not mean it cannot be done safely.

Frequently, accidents happen due to climber error, especially when the climber is a novice.

It is your responsibility to stay safe while climbing.

You are responsible for performing safety checks on yourself, as well as checking your climbing partner and vice versa.

Whether scaling cliffs or artificial walls, always make it a habit to check all personal equipment, as well as knots and devices before the ascent.

Climbing safety must be taken seriously at all times, as it is a matter of life and death.

Rope Check

Before climbing or belaying, ensure that you have the right end of the rope.

When top-rope climbing, the climber ties into the rope that is closest to the wall, while the belayer uses the end farthest out from the wall.

During the climb, always be aware of the location of the rope.

The rope should always be in front of and run over your leg or the top of your toes.

A rope behind or between the legs will cause a climber to flip upside down in a fall.

Harness Check

After you gear up and tie in, always check the safety of your harness before climbing.

To check the harness, ensure the waistbelt rests comfortably above the hips and does not slide down.

Check that the belay and leg loops are not twisted.

Leg loops should be snug around the legs.

Make sure that all buckles on the waistbelt and leg loops are fastened securely and doubled back.

After you have completed your harness safety check, have your climbing partner perform an inspection of your harness.

Finally, perform the same check on your partner's harness.

Knot Check

As discussed previously, ensuring a proper knot is paramount when it comes to climbing safety.

A poorly tied figure-eight knot can quickly come undone, slide out of the harness, and result in injury or death.

Start the check by ensuring the rope goes through both hardpoints of the harness.

Check the figure-eight follow-through used to tie in by counting five sets of two parallel lines.

Ensure the knot is tightened down close to the body and that at least two fist-lengths of tail remain.

Tie a stopper knot for backup.

Always double-check and back up any knots and anchors before climbing.

Have your climbing partner perform an inspection of your knots and anchors and execute the same check on your partner's knots and anchors.

Helmet Check

To avoid severe head injuries, always wear a helmet when climbing or belaying outdoors.

Helmets protect your head from falling rocks and fall injuries.

Make sure that the helmet sits securely on your head without sliding from side to side or backward and forward.

Ensure the helmet covers the front, back, and both sides of the head and that all buckles are securely tightened and doubled back.

Device Check

Equally important are checking belay devices and carabiners.

If you are belaying, double-check that the rope is appropriately threaded into your belay device with the brake end coming out in front of you.

Ensure that both the rope and the wire keeper of the belay device are clipped onto the carabiner.

Check that the carabiner is securely clipped to the belay loop of the harness.

Make sure the carabiner is locked and is not being cross-loaded.

Cross-loading occurs when the gate or spine of the carabiner takes the load. Cross-loading can be caused by shifting during use.

Have your climbing partner do a check of your belay set up and perform the same inspection on your partner's belay set up.

Climbing Communication

Always pay attention when belaying for a climber. The climber is the one who risks the fall and depends on you to fall safely. Use the appropriate climber and belay commands every time you belay and climb. Never allow yourself to become distracted while belaying. Never take your partner off belay until they have communicated the "off belay" command and you are confident they are safe; their life depends on it.

Safely Falling

Falling is always scary but will become more natural, the more you practice and progress.

If you feel like you are about to fall, always tell your belayer "watch me" so they can prepare and take any slack out of the line.

Similarly, say "falling" when you feel yourself coming off the wall so your belay partner can quickly lock off the rope and hold you.

The fall itself can be divided into three parts:

- Coming off the wall

- Falling

- Landing

When you feel yourself falling, breathe out to relax your body.

Keep your legs bent, and arms in front of you with elbows bent. Do not try to grab anything, as this can result in serious injury.

While falling, look down to see what is coming, but do not be tempted to push off the wall. Pushing off the wall will cause you to smack into the wall harder when you land.

> **Instead, keeping your legs bent will help you to land softly against the wall.**

Falling is going to happen; therefore, it is best to practice falling safely. Top-roping is preferred when practicing falls.

When top-roping, always ensure the rope is in front of you as you climb. Having the line in this position eliminates the risk of flipping upside down in a fall or getting rope burn.

Start at a low height and take a fall, gradually increasing the height as you feel comfortable.

Also, consider taking a falling class with a qualified instructor.

Beginner climbers must always use sound judgment, as they are the most at risk for accidents. Redundancy is a must to prevent accidents.

Always check and then double-check all climbing systems.

> **Always use gear properly as it is intended.**

> **Use equipment rated for climbing.**

Be proactive and avoid injury by removing any jewelry or accessories that could catch on the rock.

Never attempt to climb beyond your ability and skill level and never rely solely on books and tutorials to learn.

For your safety, and the security of your climbing partner, always seek help from a qualified climbing expert.

Transitioning to Outdoor Climbs

Transitioning to outdoor climbing often presents a new set of challenges to those accustomed to "pulling plastic" in an indoor gym.

These challenges often require the climber to master new skills and be more prepared.

For this reason, the new climber must seek guidance from a skilled climbing expert when transitioning to climbing outdoors.

Some climbers prefer to stay within the comfort

of the gym, while others cannot resist the call of the wild and natural rock, and some transition smoothly between the two.

For best results, it is practical to think of indoor climbing as training for outdoor climbing.

While there are numerous variables to outdoor climbing, the following are some primary considerations.

Environment

Indoor gyms offer bright lighting and climate control, but these luxuries do not exist when climbing outdoors.

> *The weather on the crag can range from hot and sunny to cold, windy, rainy, and any variation in between.*

Be prepared by dressing appropriately and consider any needs such as sun, wind, and bug protection.

Soft terrain is another luxury that does not exist outdoors.

Falling outdoors requires a slightly

higher level of skill than indoor falling.

Landings are never flat as trees and boulders may obstruct the fall line.

Likewise, there will not always be a flat floor from which to belay a climber. You may find instead you have to belay from a cliff's edge.

Always pay attention to your surroundings and be prepared for any accident.

Fear Factor

The fear factor is generally increased when transitioning from indoor to outdoor climbing; rightly so, as numerous things can go wrong while climbing.

In a gym setting, you learn the rules, pass a belay test, and have gym employees to monitor safety. None of these elements exist outdoors.

Outdoors you are in charge of the safety of yourself and partner, making it critical to pay attention.

Always climb with a partner you trust.

There are several things you can do to help decrease feelings of fear.

- Always check and double-check all climbing systems before use.

- Never allow yourself to become distracted while belaying.

- Evaluate any fixed gear and do not use any equipment you feel is unstable or unsecured.

A fear of falling is commonly increased outdoors, as there is a higher risk.

Practice falling frequently to help control anxiety about falling outdoors.

Although it may feel unnatural to come off the wall, frequent training will prepare you to know what to do when you fall.

Practice falls also help take the edge off as you gain more experience.

Gear

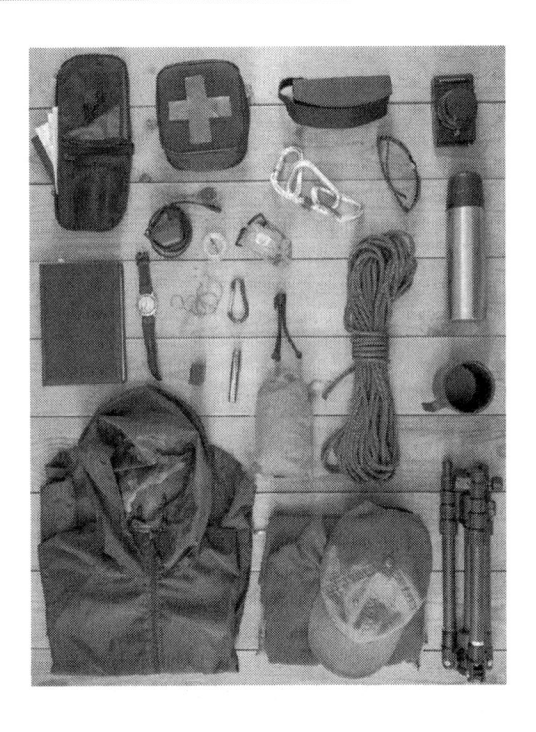

The kind of gear you need will depend on the type of climb and the location.

Climbing outdoor routes requires the climber to evaluate how much equipment is needed.

Always bring enough gear for climbing. In most cases, it is better to bring too much rather than too little.

Become familiar with reading guidebooks, which tell you how

much gear you will need.

In addition to climbing gear, consider taking equipment as if you were going camping overnight.

This gear includes items like flashlights, water, food, and a first-aid kit.

Also, be sure to dress in layers, as weather conditions can quickly change.

It is better to have to carry a slightly heavier pack than not be prepared.

Grades

Indoor climbing grades do not correspond to outdoor climbing grades.

While you may have no problem climbing a 5.11a in the gym, you may struggle climbing a 5.8 outdoors.

Do not let this get you down.

Outdoor climbs are not adorned with colorful holds to direct your route and real rock feels much different than plastic.

Every outdoor climb is different and requires the climber to adapt to each one. To familiarize yourself with outdoor grades, warm up with accessible routes.

Get a feel for the rock and repeat the routes as many times as you need to feel comfortable.

Never try to climb beyond your ability or skill level.

Helmet

Helmets are often depicted as looking "dorky," but wearing a helmet any time you climb or belay outside is critical.

Helmets protect your head from injury in a fall and prevent damage from falling rocks and boulders.

If a rock is falling, be sure to shout "ROCK" to your belayer and anyone below.

While you will find climber's who opt for no helmet, no one will make fun of you for choosing to be safe.

Holds

Without a brightly-colored path to mark the route of ascent, it becomes more challenging to zip up a climb.

Take your time and work slowly.

Climbing outdoors requires learning to look for natural hand and footholds, often unmarked.

It takes time and experience to recognize what kinds of holds work well.

Respect Nature (and Each Other)

When climbing outdoors, it is your responsibility to respect nature and abide by climbing etiquette.

Always practice the "pack it in, pack it out" rule.

Pack out any trash, food, and equipment.

Be respectful of the wildlife, flora, or fauna.

Be mindful of cleaning chalk marks and keeping your climbing gear contained to one area.

Climbing in small groups is recommended, as large groups can put a strain on limited routes.

Unlike climbing gyms, do not play loud music or yell and curse. Instead, respect the area by talking softly and not yelling or cursing.

Be courteous of fellow climbers and appreciate the space you share.

Last Word about Outdoor Climbing

No matter how much indoor experience you have, your first climb outdoors will present challenges.

Always climb with an experienced partner, whether it be a seasoned climber or an instructor.

Never climb above your skill level or do anything in which you do not feel confident.

The only way to become better outdoors is to practice climbing outdoors. As you gain experience, you also increase confidence.

Advancing Your Climbing Skills

Every climber, at some point, has to decide to advance in skill level.

You may find yourself crushing 5.6 routes, eager to take on 5.8, or you may find it challenging to complete a 5.6 with ease.

No matter which category you fall in, you will need to decide on how to advance.

How quickly you improve has many variables and is different for each climber.

While it may not be what most beginners want to hear, progressing to more difficult grades can sometimes take years.

When deciding how to advance, understanding what you want to achieve is an excellent place to start.

Whether you enjoy indoor recreational climbing or you envision yourself scaling walls in Yosemite, both options are acceptable.

Set climbing goals that are tailored to match what you wish to achieve.

Understand that there will be both success and failure and allow yourself the opportunity to improve over time steadily.

Going to the Next Level

The following are simple tips to help take your climbing to the next level:

Climb

As previously stated, the only way to get better at climbing is to climb and climb often. Do lots of easy climbs and do them well.

Try out different movements, hand, and footholds. Work on technique, endurance, and activities that give you trouble.

Set up a routine climbing schedule that helps you reach your established goals.

It is essential to maintain consistency in how much you climb every week to build a solid foundation as a climber.

Rest days are necessary, but practicing every week will yield better results than taking a few weeks off.

Yearn to Learn

Have an eagerness to learn. Watch other climbers, how they move and approach a route.

Climb with people on lower and equal skill levels, and if possible, climb with those of higher skills levels.

Ask questions about anything you do not understand.

More advanced climbers can offer tips, guidance, and advice on how to complete challenging routes and problems.

Push Yourself

It can be easy to settle into a routine of climbing easy routes.

Climbing accessible routes over and over are great for practice, but will never allow for grade improvement.

After you master an easy climb, start choosing routes that present more of a challenge and require more effort and focus.

Avoid giving up after one or two fails. Instead, give your body time to adjust to the wall to really put forth an effort.

You will never know what climbing skills you can achieve if you fail to try.

Try Different Styles

After you feel confident with top-roping, try learning a different style, such as single-pitch sport climbing.

Many rock gyms and recreational stores like REI offer next-level classes to go from a beginner climber to intermediate.

Not ready to go outdoors yet? Try going to another local gym with new routes.

> *Also, try new rock types, like sandstone and granite.*

Climbing on different types of rock requires different footwork.

The variety in the kind of climbing and the kind of rock will improve your technique by allowing you to try new holds and moves.

Continuing Education

The number of books and online resources for rock climbing is seemingly endless. If you have trouble with or do not understand specific climbing details, seek out either of these for reference. While these items are great resources, never solely rely on books and online tutorials for climbing. Many climbers share bad habits or methods that are not entirely safe. Likewise, reading a book or online article does not make you qualified or give you hands-on experience. For your safety and the safety of others, always seek help and guidance from a skilled, experienced climber when looking to advance your skills.

Conclusion

Heart racing, legs trembling, palms damp with sweat, you cling to the side of the wall in search of the next hold, the next foot placement that will advance you higher. You catch a glimpse of the distance below as your brain confronts you with all the things that could go wrong.

"I will probably fall..."

With every move you fight against your mind, every cell in your body screaming.

"...but I know how to do it right."

You reach the top; your tiny size put into context against the giant walls.

You feel powerful, humbled, free. In this inspired instant, you realize that it is not always about the climb itself, but what you learned about yourself on the way up.

"I am stronger now than ever. I am courageous. I completed this goal!"

* * * * * * * *

There is no magic pill or quick solution to becoming a more advanced climber. Efficient movement and precise footwork take years to develop.

Allow yourself time to make mistakes and learn from them. Always act responsibly and practice climbing safely.

More importantly, remember to have fun and enjoy the view.

No matter where your climbing journey may take you, it is only up from here.

Thank you for reading this book. It has been refreshing to record in one book what I have learned in my own journey while learning how to climb.

I am still learning, adapting, and experimenting with my own limits. Climbing, for me, as I said, has been more about the overall experience and not just in the success of accessing the summit.

If this book has helped you, inspired you, or educated you in any way, would you please consider leaving a review wherever you purchased this book? I do actually read all of the reviews and take them to heart to improve my writing skills.

Remember, it's all about the journey, not the destination.

Happy trails!

Made in the USA
Las Vegas, NV
21 July 2024